Iain D. Campbell's 'Heroes aed
and breathtaking panorama of ry
of the church with observati er.
How important that we do n We
learn history's lessons not in ves
for what happened long ago but to unde~~~~~, to
appreciate God's providence and salvation and better honour Jesus
Christ as the Lord of all nations. Let's take responsibility for the present
and build on the insights of those heroes who went before us. Let's
also learn from past heresies so that we don't repeat those errors.

Geoffrey Thomas
Minister of Alfred Place Baptist Church, Aberystwyth

Christians unaware of the history of Christianity are likely to be
unhealthily rootless. Iain Campbell's century-by-century survey keeps
its eye chiefly on developments of concern to conservative and Scottish
believers. It is a very helpful tool for equipping oneself with knowledge
of what God was doing in earlier eras, and hence for understanding
what he is doing worldwide today.

David F Wright
Professor Emeritus of Patristic & Reformed Christianity
University of Edinburgh

In an age where Christians are increasingly ignorant of their historical
roots, Dr Campbell has done us a great service by achieving the near
impossible: covering 2 000 years of church history in twenty brief but
highly informative chapters. A great place to start for anyone who
wants to deepen their understanding of how the church has witnessed
to christ throughout the ages.

Carl Trueman
Associate Professor of Church History
Westminster Theological Seminary

HEROES&
HERETICS

PIVOTAL MOMENTS IN 20 CENTURIES OF THE CHURCH

IAIN D. CAMPBELL

CHRISTIAN FOCUS

© Iain D. Campbell 2004

ISBN 1-85792-925-X

Published in 2004
by
Christian Focus Publications, Geanies House,
Fearn, Ross-shire, IV20 1TW, Scotland

www.christianfocus.com

Cover design by Alister Macinnes

Printed and bound by
Mackays of Chatham

Contents

Dedicated to the members and adherents
of the Free Church of Scotland, Back, Isle of Lewis

'A seed shall serve him'
Psalm 22:30

Preface

In August 1999 I began a series of twenty half-hour lectures in my congregation, in addition to our weekly schedule of services. These lectures formed a kind of 'millennium project', as we spent the closing months of the twentieth century reflecting on two thousand years of Christian history. My intention was to lecture each week on a successive century of church history, covering all twenty before the second millennium closed.

The lectures concluded on schedule at the end of December 1999 (with a little re-arranging of the timetable at points in between). I owe my congregation my thanks for their support and encouragement, and for their interest in attending the lectures. I hope they learned something from them.

The following chapters have been written on the basis of these lectures. Specialists may complain that the chapters are too general; generalists may find fault with what I have included and what I have, on other occasions, omitted. I have tried to be extensive without generalising too much, but I have also given disproportionate emphasis in the latter part of the book to events in Scotland. I have also laid emphasis on what Mark Noll would call 'turning points', events which were of pivotal importance, such as the Reformation and the Puritan movements. I have tried to tell that story in a manner that is interesting and, I hope, useful.

The introduction was originally part of the first lecture, but I considered it necessary to separate it from that chapter, which has been slightly modified. The story of the Church's attempt to fulfil the Great Commission of Matthew 28:19 and to 'make disciples' is unending. What Christ began 'to do and to teach' has already given the church a history, and that story will continue until God's elect are gathered into his kingdom. Then the story will culminate and climax in eternity, where it will never end.

A work of this kind necessarily draws heavily on more detailed studies. If the number of footnotes is out of proportion to the length of the work, that is because I considered it necessary to list sources of information in many instances. The number of notes is a measure of my dependence on others, and I hope that the material in the notes will stimulate further reading. Rather than publish a standard bibliography, I have supplemented the books listed in footnotes with a list of books for further reading. These again indicate works that I have found most useful. I have tried to include a brief chronology at the beginning of every chapter to give a framework for the events that took place during that particular century. Many dates are tentative, and published histories do not always agree on the dates of people's lives.

I should like to record a special thanks to all those who stayed behind on all of these weeks of 1999 after our weekly prayer meetings to listen to the lectures with enthusiasm and interest. Once again I owe much thanks to the editorial work of Mr Malcolm Maclean at Christian Focus Publications, and to those who suggested changes to the manuscript. Above all, I would like to thank, once again, my wife and family for their unfailing support and prayers every time I make the journey from my study to my pulpit. Physically it is a short walk; but only they know how long it can sometimes be. Their constant love is my great inspiration to make it at all. I dedicate this book to the congregation in which it has been my privilege to minister God's Word since 1995, with the prayer that many more disciples will be made through the preaching of the gospel in the Free Church of Scotland congregation of Back in the Isle of Lewis.

This is the story of Jesus' work, beginning with these far-off days when he walked this earth. First-century Palestine is far removed from twenty-first-century Britain. And yet the gospel Jesus preached then continues to be preached now. He calls men to serve him, and to devote their energies to making him known. May that gospel continue to inspire all those who have remained faithful to the sacred trust to go into all the world and make disciples of all nations.

Iain D. Campbell
Back Free Church of Scotland
September 2003

Introduction

When my family and I visited Detroit, USA, in April 1999, we took a trip to the Henry Ford Museum in Greenfield, Michigan. The Museum stands as a powerful testimony to the resourcefulness of a young man who transformed America's motor industry. Ford was only 15 when he built his first internal combustion engine, and at the age of 33 he built his first car. There is ample testimony to his ability in the number of cars on our roads which bear his surname!

In 1919, at the end of Ford's first period as president of the Ford Motor Company, he was involved in a libel lawsuit against the *Chicago Tribune*. While on the stand during the course of his trial, Ford uttered the following assessment of history: 'History,' he said, 'is more or less bunk.'

Despite the fact that Ford encouraged education and established a museum, his words could be taken as a dismissal of the rich legacy of the past. Perhaps some people share his view, believing that the dawn of a new millennium is not a time for looking back. Yet it is of supreme importance that we look back on this most significant of anniversaries, two thousand years after the Incarnation, and remind ourselves of the great works of God in history. The Christian, of all people, cannot regard history as bunk.

The Christian philosophy of history

For the Christian, history is rich with meaning. We must never despise it. It is not nonsense. There was once a movement which was called deism; the deists believed that although God had made the world, he was not interested in it afterwards. He made it, then left it. The world was created with potential, and God, deism says, left it to fulfil its potential. But if this is true, then history is no more than the sum of individual experiences, and life has no meaning. On the other hand, the Christian believes that God, in his works of Providence, is intimately concerned with the world at every stage of its development, and with history in its evolution. Because of this, we have a threefold view of history.

First, Christians believe that God is the *author* of history. The *Westminster Confession of Faith* reminds us that God is an intelligent, personal Being, who has foreordained whatsoever comes to pass. As A.A. Hodge says in his *Commentary on the Confession*, 'No event is isolated, either in the physical or moral world, either in heaven or in earth.'[1] When R.L. Dabney was installed as Professor of Ecclesiastical History in Virginia in 1854, he gave an inaugural lecture on the 'Uses and Results of Church History' in which he laid down the principle that

> the history of the church and of the world, regarded as a whole, is but the evolution of the eternal purpose of that God who 'worketh all things after the counsel of his own will'. Deep in the secrets of his own breast is hid the united plan, from which the pattern is gradually unfolded on the tangled web of human affairs. As that decree is one, so history is a unit.[2]

Dabney concluded that 'no man but the believer is capable of understanding the philosophy of history'.[3] Dabney is not saying that an unbeliever cannot be a historian, or even a church historian; even an atheist may be capable of researching and recording the facts of history. But the believer understands the meaning of history, because he puts God first and acknowledges the divine hand that is at work in the events of life.

Second, the Christian believes that 'the redemptive purpose of God lies at the centre of this world's history'.[4] All that occurs in the world takes place in order that sinners might be redeemed; history becomes the scaffolding around the construction of the church. Reviewing a life full of unexpected events and strange providences, Joseph could say that 'God meant it for good, *in order to bring it about as it is this day, to save many people alive*' (Gen. 50:20). To put it another way, God's common grace, extended to all men, always serves the purpose of special, saving grace. The events of this world's history set the stage upon which the drama of redemption is enacted.

Third, the Christian believes that the outworking of history is intimately related to the Person of Jesus Christ as King of Kings and Lord of Lords. He is to have the pre-eminence in all things. Paul could say that all things in Heaven and earth were for him, and by him, and consist in him. Jesus stands *over* history as its Lord, *behind* history as its meaning, and *before* history as its purpose.

This is true of all history, and it is the only framework within which we can view the events that take place in the world.

The Christian view of church history

But there is a special branch of historical study which is concerned with the study of church history, with the development and growth of the Christian faith. Just as Scotland has its history, as the Royal Family has its history, as the United Nations has a history, the church has its history too. We stand in these opening months of the new millennium at a very significant point, where twenty centuries of church history have gone by, and if we are to understand where we are and where we are going, we must understand where we have come from.

Church history tells the story of the establishment and consolidation of Christian groups and congregations, their growth and, in many cases, their decline; it embraces the development of Christian thought and the evolution of Christian doctrine; it embraces the biographies of the great men whom God raised up at specific times and specific periods to guide and direct and teach the church in order that his truth might be maintained. William Cunningham reminds us that the Roman Catholic view of church history is that Christ intended to have a society which would remain infallible and free from error. The Protestant view, on the other hand, is that Christ had no such intention:

> there is no evidence in Scripture that Christ intended to preserve a widely extended, perpetually visible society upon earth, which should always be free from all error; and still less that He intended to confer this privilege upon the Church of Rome; and that, therefore, the promises of His presence and Spirit do not secure it.[5]

Nor are we to believe, as some modern writers argue, that church history is merely a secular science with a theological interest, as if we can look at the history of the church as we look at the history of a secular institution.[6] Church history is the story of God's preservation of his truth and the gathering in of sinners into his kingdom through that truth. In other words, the gospel has two dimensions in its operation in this world: the theological dimension and the historical dimension. It is through the truth of God's Word that sinners are saved. We need a theology, we need to know what the truth is, to formulate it in a biblical manner and in biblical proportion. We also need to know the limits of theological enquiry – where does theological enquiry start? Where does it end? What are its sources? What is its dynamic?

But we also need to know our history. Dr D. Martyn Lloyd-Jones has an interesting lecture on this theme in the compilation *The Puritans – their Origins and Successors*. The lecture is entitled 'Can we learn from history?' He argues not only that we can, but that we must. He says:

> My argument is that it is always essential for us to supplement our reading of theology with the reading of church history. Or, if you prefer it, that we should at any rate take our theology in an historical manner. If we do not, we shall be in danger of becoming abstract, theoretical, and academic in our view of truth; and, failing to relate it to the practicalities of life and daily living, we shall soon be in trouble.[7]

Church history is important because there we see the outworking of God's truth in man's life, truth for life, theology that cannot be divorced from the events that shape our thinking and our living.

At the same time, we must remember that history is, to a large extent, a matter of interpretation. When we deal with biblical material, such as the historical material in the Books of Kings, or in the Gospel narratives, we are dealing with documents inspired by the Holy Spirit. When we read subsequent church history, we are dependent on human writings, and we make fallible judgements. And, in spite of all I have said about God as the author of history, we must also remember that he has hidden from our view much of what he has been doing in and through the church. The story of the church is unending; it is also a story which is truly known only to God. There are always limits to our inquiry.

My intention in this series of studies is to look consecutively at each succeeding century of church history. It will soon become clear that there are some centuries of far greater significance than others, and some centuries in which there was more development of thought and religious ideas than others. There is a disproportionate significance to some centuries. William Cunningham, for example, suggested that 'the first four centuries after the apostolic age ... are invested with no small measure of interest and importance with respect to the history of theology'.[8] Also, no one would doubt the significance of the fifteenth, sixteenth and seventeenth centuries and the massive impact of the Reformation on church life and on theological reflection. But I think it is important that we have a general picture. I do not want to particularise, but to generalise, not to specialise in the history of Presbyterianism or Protestantism, but to highlight and learn from the major movements of church history since the first century. So let us begin at the beginning.

The First Century – Beginnings

Important dates

33	Jesus is crucified
45–64	Missionary Journeys of Paul
70	Jerusalem is destroyed by the Romans
94	The emperor Domitian begins his persecution of Christians

The first century of church history is really the period covered by the New Testament. In one sense it is the century with which Christians are most familiar, even if in chronological terms it is the most remote from us. Its thought patterns meet ours constantly in the reading of the New Testament. We move in the world and atmosphere of first-century Palestine, and we are familiar with its social customs and habits, as well as its thought patterns, as we follow the life and ministry of Jesus and his disciples. By doing so, our faith is strengthened, as we listen to the teachings of the Man of Galilee, who lived during the first thirty years of the century, and shaped the destiny of the world for ever. Within a hundred years of his birth the Bible will have been written. The first evangelists will have gone out with a message of salvation for all men, and the gospel will be impacting societies and cultures far removed from the circles in which Jesus lived and taught. That story is the beginning of our study. But first we need to explore the background to the New Testament.

Background
Paul tells us, in Galatians 4:4, that Jesus was born 'in the fullness of the time'. That is, God prepared the world for his coming. This preparation involved three different historical and cultural strands, which lie behind the New Testament and form the backdrop to the

15

events of the first century. These strands of influence colour the New Testament world, and give us a perspective from which to view the life and teaching of Jesus Christ.

First, there is the Jewish background. This is the most important, because it was through the Jewish race, the sons of Abraham, that God had revealed himself and had made known the promise of the coming Messiah. As J. Gresham Machen puts it:

> Christianity was not an entirely new religion. It was rooted in the divine revelation already given to the chosen people. Even those things which were most distinctive of Christianity had been foreshadowed in Old Testament prophecy. Salvation was of the Jews.[9]

The Aramaic language, a linguistic successor of Hebrew, was the spoken language of the Jews of Palestine, and the religious heritage of the Jews focused on the temple and on the synagogue.

When Jesus preached his gospel message, he made it clear that he had not come to destroy God's previous revelation, but to fulfil it. He taught the gospel out of the Old Testament Scriptures, and demonstrated that the whole Old Testament spoke about himself. He had come as the promised Saviour, the promised Messiah. Just as Jewish blood ran in Jesus' veins, the Jewish Scriptures filled his soul and gave meaning to his life's work and mission.[10] As a result, something new was being built on the foundation of the Old Testament. Consequently, we find a dualism in New Testament teaching which asserts on the one hand all that the early church owed to Judaism (and all that Jesus owed to his Jewishness), and which asserts on the other hand that something better than Judaism has come. We are the children of Abraham as we are the followers of Jesus.

Second, there is a Roman background to the New Testament. When the New Testament opens, Palestine is under the domination of the Roman Empire. About 50 years before Christ, Rome had become dominant among the cities of the world. In 48 BC Julius Caesar had acquired supreme power. The Caesars were to retain imperial sway in Palestine throughout the New Testament history; by the time the first century closes, Jerusalem, the holy city of David, had been destroyed by Rome. Although Rome was to persecute many Christians, the imperial power was also used by God to spread the gospel. For example, the influence of Roman civilisation, seen in the infrastructure of roads that had been built and in improved means of communication, meant that there was a mechanism in place for making Christ's message known all over the world. Had it not been for the Roman influence, the gospel could never have flourished as it did.

Third, there is the Greek background. The Greek civilisation was one of the wonders of the ancient world, which bequeathed a rich legacy of literature and of philosophy. Greek had become a dominant language, and it became the language in which the New Testament was written, a universal language which could be read and understood by the intellectuals as well as by the common man. In the course of the New Testament, Paul confronted that Greek world with the gospel as he preached in important and strategic centres like Athens and Corinth, urging men to love and serve Christ. Indeed, it was after hearing a Greek man calling for help in making the gospel known that Paul turned the course of the gospel towards Europe (Acts 16:9-10). Those of us who live and serve in Western Europe owe that Macedonian man our very souls!

The life of Christ

It was into this social, political and religious world that Jesus was born. Our knowledge of him comes from the records we have in the Gospels. Some modern scholars believe that the Gospels were largely written under later (Pauline) influence for a theological purpose; consequently, it is suggested, they are limited in their usefulness as history. Another school of thought was of the opinion that it is impossible for us to know much of the historical Jesus. The supernatural, miraculous element of the New Testament writings, it was alleged, had hidden the historical person of Nazareth from our view. Scholars like Rudolf Bultmann said that since most of the New Testament record is mythical, in the sense that modern science regards its worldview as untenable, we can have little knowledge about Jesus and first-century Palestinian Judaism. This approach sought to divide between the Jesus of history and the Christ of faith, as if the Christ whom the church preached and believed in was somehow other than the Jesus of Nazareth, the historical person. Others highlight the apparent discrepancies in the Gospel records to show that it really is impossible to have an accurate historical life of Christ.

Some more recent scholars, however, have argued that we can, in fact, know a great deal about Jesus, and that the portrait that we find in the Gospels is accurate.[11] Evangelical Christians, therefore, accept that the Gospels give us a historical record and that the details given there of the life of Jesus are accurate in themselves, and may be supplemented from extra-biblical accounts. Coupled with this is the obvious fact that the Gospels were not written to give biographical information but to serve the interests of the gospel message of the New Testament church.[12] Clearly also the different Gospel writers wrote for different purposes and different audiences. This being so, the remarkable thing is that the Gospels show such a coherence of historical fact, and give us a full picture of the ministry of Christ. There is a concentration on the last three years of Jesus' life; and within this period there is a disproportionate emphasis on his trial, sufferings, death and resurrection. There is much we do not know; but what we do know is enough for us.

Jesus was born into an ordinary (and poor) Jewish home, the child of Joseph, a carpenter, and his wife, Mary. We know that Mary was expecting this, her first child, when she actually married Joseph; the Jews threw it at Jesus on one occasion that he was an illegitimate child (John 8:41). But we also know that the conception of Jesus had been nothing short of miraculous: the Holy Spirit had 'overshadowed' Mary, and in that moment the eternal Son of God, for that is who Jesus was, became man. Jesus existed before he was conceived; and in his conception – his incarnation (becoming flesh) – he became like us, entering our world, and sharing our pain.

The Gospels do not go into great detail about the life of Christ. There is evidence to suggest, however, that by the time Jesus did become a public herald of God's kingdom, Joseph had died, leaving him responsible for Mary and the rest of the family. By this time he had become a professional carpenter like Joseph before him (Mark 6:3).

At the commencement of his ministry, Jesus was baptised by John the Baptist, a strange figure who appeared out of the desert, preaching that the Messiah – the Saviour whom God had promised in the Old Testament – was about to come. When John saw Jesus, he publicly declared that this was the Lamb of God who would take away the sins of the world (John 1:29). At the baptism of Jesus, too, God declared that this was his Son, and that he was pleased with his work (Matthew 3:13-17). Jesus was baptised with the Holy Spirit, and equipped in a new way for the new work that lay before him.

Jesus spent three years proclaiming that the Kingdom of God had come. He was the promised Saviour. The Old Testament Scriptures, he declared, spoke about him. The Old Testament church had waited for him. Now God was going to do a great work, for the salvation of sinners, through Jesus' death and resurrection. Jesus showed proof of this in performing miracles – supernatural works which gave proof of his unique office and messianic work. He healed the sick, commanded the elements of nature, and raised the dead to life. He also called disciples to accompany him; they were chosen not only to assist him in his work, but also as those who would be used to tell the Jesus story and lay the foundation of the New Testament church. To those who accompanied him during his lifetime, Jesus would add Paul. Through these men, the teachings of Jesus would go on being taught long after his ascension to Heaven.

The teaching of Jesus offended the Jewish religious leaders. They resented the fact that Jesus had had no theological training, and that he appeared to be setting himself up as an expert and judge. Their growing hostility led at last to a trial before the Roman governor, Pilate, and subsequently to his condemnation and crucifixion. Death by crucifixion was long and agonising. For six hours Jesus hung on the cross, until at last he died. We know that during that period he was engaging with God as the sin-bearer, dying for the needs of men and women.

Jesus died at Passover time. On the first day of the following week, it was discovered that his grave was empty. Despite all the attempts to guard it, his body was not there. The disciples were amazed, until it became clear that Jesus had actually risen from the dead! Pilate had tried to make sure that the body could not be robbed by anyone breaking *into* the grave; he had not reckoned on the dead man breaking *out* of the grave! The message of the resurrection gave hope and life and encouragement to the early church. It was central to their preaching. Without it, there could be no good news.

But here was the climax of all that Jesus had come to be and to do. He had destroyed sin and its power by going right into death and coming out alive and victorious.

B.B. Warfield, in his excellent work *The Lord of Glory*, summarises in this way:

> Here is a young man scarcely thirty-three years of age, emerged from obscurity only for the brief space of three years, living during those years under the scorn of the world, which grew steadily in intensity and finally passed into hatred, and dying at the end the death of a malefactor: but leaving behind Him the germs of a world-wide community, the spring of whose vitality is the firm conviction that He was God manifest in the flesh ... apart from evidence so convincing, the high claims of Jesus could not have been met with such firm and unquestioning faith by His followers. This very faith becomes thus a proof of the truth of his claims.[13]

Following his physical departure to Heaven, forty days after the resurrection, Jesus left behind the apostolic band which had accompanied him during his ministry. Around AD 33, the Holy Spirit was poured upon them in a small room in Jerusalem. Just as Jesus himself had been equipped for his ministry and service, so he now equipped his disciples for the task of evangelising the whole world. His words to them were, 'You will be my witnesses in Jerusalem and all Judea and in Samaria, and to the ends of the earth' (Acts 1:8). Thus the Jesus movement, the Christian church of the New Testament age, was born.

The growth and consolidation of the church

The first great preacher of the New Testament church was Peter, who was to have a specific ministry to the Jews of the dispersion. The early church was built first in areas to which Jews had been scattered, and their synagogues and Hebrew Scriptures were used to demonstrate that Messiah had indeed come, and that Jesus was the promised Saviour. Despite the fact that Rome began almost immediately to vent its anger on the early church, the flames of persecution only served to spread the gospel further.

Following the work of Christ one of the greatest moments in the history of the first century church was the conversion of Saul of Tarsus. A Roman citizen, whose family belonged to a strict sect of Judaism (he says of himself in Acts 23:6 that he was 'a Pharisee and the son of a Pharisee'), he had received his schooling and training from Gamaliel, a leading Jerusalem rabbi. Implacably hostile in his early years to Christ and Christianity, he was born again dramatically in about AD 35, while travelling to Damascus in order to imprison and persecute Christians there. Instead, he too met with the living Christ, and ended his journey worshipping with the Christians whom he had come to persecute. Understandably, some were suspicious that he was not a true Christian at all. But God proved these suspicions unfounded, and for the next thirty years it was chiefly Paul whom God used for the expansion of the church. The Council of Jerusalem in AD 49 recognised that God was sending the gospel to the Gentiles, and Paul was set apart for that purpose.

From around 45 the New Testament books began to be written, with some of the Pauline epistles among the earliest of these. This process of inscripturation continued until the Book of Revelation was written around 95, thus closing the canon of Scripture, and giving the church, in the space of some sixty years after the death of Jesus, a record both of the life and teaching of Christ, and, through the letters of the New Testament, an explanation of the meaning and significance of his death and resurrection. God also gave the church guidance as to how it should be regulated in worship and in practice.

The church government of the New Testament was simple, with church officers divided into bishops and deacons. The function of the bishops or elders was spiritual, and was concerned with rule, discipline and teaching. The function of the deacons was practical; in the first instance they were to ensure that financial contributions to the work of the church were evenly distributed among those who had the greatest need. The worship was based on the synagogue worship whose praise-book was the Old Testament Psalter.

By the end of the first century the original apostles had all died. Although the New Testament says little about how they met their end, tradition has it that most were martyred for their faith, Thomas being martyred in India, Bartholomew in Armenia, Andrew in Achaia (Greece) and both Paul and Peter at Rome during Nero's persecution of Christians in AD 64. From their original role as a group dedicated to following Jesus they were separated from one another and were used in various ways to bring the gospel to different parts of the world. They represent for us the missionary work and endeavour of the church in every age and in every place. They also leave us the example of putting the gospel first before life itself.

So, despite the weakness of the apostles themselves, and despite the many persecutions which arose, the gospel flourished and the church continued to grow. Empowered by the Holy Spirit, and directed by the Head of the church, the apostles laid the foundation on which we build still. The advance of the Jesus movement was quite staggering in its early stages. Historian A.M. Renwick says that

> by the end of the first century, the gospel had been carried far from its starting-point in Jerusalem. No amount of persecution could stop it. Towards the East it had reached Mesopotamia and Parthia. In the West it had spread to Gaul and Spain. The Church was growing already in the great cities of Rome, Alexandria and Carthage. In Antioch and Ephesus as well as in Corinth, it was very strong. Christian groups were to be found scattered throughout Syria, Arabia and Illyria. Such was the record of seventy years' work in the face of constant opposition.[14]

The Second Century – Expansion

Important dates

120   Growth of the Gnostic movement
144   Death of Marcion
155   Martyrdom of Polycarp of Smyrna
165   Martyrdom of Justin Martyr
178   Irenaeus, Bishop of Lyons
197   Tertullian flourishes

With the second century we enter into the period known as the era of the apostolic fathers. This is the name given to men who were born before the original apostles died, and whom God raised up to continue the work of maintaining, proclaiming, and especially, as we shall see, defending the gospel. This period is not widely documented, and much of the information we have concerning the second century is taken from a few surviving writings and some incidental references in later works. The lack of hard evidence is a barrier to our knowing precisely what went on in different places after the apostles died, and prevents us from finding answers to some questions we would like to ask about the worship of Jesus in the post New Testament period.

There is another difficulty. From older church historians like William Cunningham to modern historians like Mark Noll[15] we are cautioned against the different readings of church history that have emerged in the church. A Roman Catholic reading of history, for example, tries to demonstrate that there was a direct linear succession from the apostles through the bishops of Rome, who kept the church pure by an infallible and inerrant tradition. The Eastern Orthodox churches argue that the church was kept pure through its confessions, councils and liturgies. Evangelical Protestants, in affirming the apostolic authority of the New Testament, say that these writings were foundational and were applied by succeeding generations of Christians.

They also argue that there is no such thing as a completely pure church. God alone knows who are true Christians, and that he has had witnesses and faithful servants in every age and generation. As we read the history of the church, therefore, we remind ourselves that only God is without error!

The canon of Scripture

Recognising the canon of the New Testament was one of the problems faced by the generation of believers after the apostles. The word 'canon' originally meant a reed, which in turn came to be used as a standard of measurement. This subsequently came to be applied to the Bible as the standard, or measure, of the church's faith and practice. During the second century the church struggled with the question of which books were to be regarded as canonical and authoritative for the church in her evangelisation of the world. During the course of the century, the apostolic fathers quote from the books of the New Testament, but it is evident from their writings that other documents and manuscripts were also in circulation.

Interestingly, it is from the writings of a second-century heretic by the name of Marcion that we know which books were being regarded as canonical. Marcion was a Gnostic (we shall come to this term later) who repudiated the Old Testament in its entirety and also some of the books which the Christians regarded as authoritative. There is also another fragment, called the Muratorian Fragment, which dates from about 175, and which lists about twenty New Testament books which were regarded as canonical. The fragment is named after the antiquarian Muratori who published it in the eighteenth century, but the original author is unknown.

Criteria for judging the canonicity of the books of Scripture included apostolicity (was it written by an apostle?), antiquity (did it go back to the apostolic era?), orthodoxy (did it accord with the apostolic faith?), lection (was it widely used and read throughout the church?) and inspiration (was it inspired?).[16] These of course do not settle every question, and it was to be some time before the church acknowledged, at a fourth century council, which books were to be regarded as authoritative. We must remind ourselves, here, of the emphasis of the Westminster Confession of Faith, that the authority of the Bible does not depend on the testimony of the church, but depends wholly upon God. We do not believe the Bible to be the inspired Word of God because the church tells us; rather the church is mandated to acknowledge as authoritative the books God has marked out as inspired. It is inspiration that leads to and establishes canonicity, not the other way round.

D.A. Hagner, in an article on the apostolic fathers, puts it like this:

In summary, the apostolic fathers provide a unique glimpse of the state of the OT and NT canons during the fifty-year period beginning toward the end of the first century ... While it is clear that the Gospels are already around in the early second century, it seems that there was a preference to quote the words of Jesus from an ongoing oral tradition. With this comes an impressive substantiation of the importance and stability of the Gospel tradition.[17]

Roman Emperors in the New Testament Age

Augustus	30BC–AD14	Referred to in Luke 2:1
Tiberius	AD 14–37	Luke 3:1
Caligula	37–41	
Claudius	41–54	Acts 11:28; 18:2
Nero	54–68	Paul's trial (Acts 25:10-12; 26:32; 28:19; 2 Timothy 4:16-17)
Galba	68	
Otto	69	
Vitellius	69	
Vespasian	69–79	Destruction of Jerusalem occurred in 70
Titus	79–81	
Domitian	81–96	
Nerva	96–98	
Trajan	98–117	

From Merrill C. Tenney's *New Testament Survey*

The apostolic fathers

Who were these apostolic fathers? We know them through some of the writings that survive (remarkably) from this period. These writings include:

- *The Letter of Clement*, which was written around 96 by Clement, a Presbyter/Elder/Bishop of the church in Rome. The letter was written to try to solve a dispute in the church at Corinth.

- *The Letters of Ignatius of Antioch*, which were written at the beginning of the century. Ignatius was executed in Rome in about 110, and he wrote seven letters to various churches as he travelled to Rome.

- *The Didache* (the word means 'teaching'), which is described as 'the oldest surviving handbook of church discipline'.[18] Part One is about Christian doctrine; Part Two about Church practice.

- *The Fragments of Papias*, which were written between 110-30. Papias was bishop of the church in Hierapolis in Phrygia. His letters were intended to preserve some of the sayings of Jesus which have not been recorded in the Gospels. Not everyone in the church accepted that these sayings were genuine.

- *The Letter of Barnabas* (c.120), which was probably written in Alexandria, and is markedly anti-Jewish. It reflects anti-Semitism in the early church, regarding the Jews merely as the murderers of Jesus.

- *The Shepherd of Hermas* (between 100 and 140), which was written in Rome. It is a strange document, in which Hermas claimed to have received revelation from two heavenly figures. Its main emphasis is on the need for moral purity in the church.

- *The Letter of Polycarp to the Philippians*, which was written about 110. Polycarp was a famous second-century martyr, and his letter is important as an indicator of mainstream church life in this period. Polycarp quotes far and wide from the New Testament writings, and warns against heresy.

- *The Letter to Diognetus*, which was written in the first half of the second century, and demonstrated the superiority of Christianity. It was a magnificent piece of writing, but the identity of the writer is unknown.

Why are these important?[19]

- *They show the spread of Christianity in the era after the apostles.* The fragments and the writings which have come down to us enable us to pinpoint the location of the emerging Christian churches and congregations. Christ had commissioned his disciples to go into all the earth with the gospel, and in the period after the New Testament, we see the church doing exactly that. The early generation of believers made remarkable progress in covering much ground with the gospel of Jesus Christ. In difficult circumstances, and often at great personal cost, the early Christians pursued the evangelisation of the world faithfully and successfully.

- *They show the nature of local church life in the era after the apostles.* Most of these documents were occasional, sent to particular churches at particular times. That is part of their usefulness, for they bear testimony to the nature of church life: how believers were organised, how they worshipped, and what they actually believed. We see that there were bishops (or presbyters) and deacons in the church. The nature of their offices is somewhat obscure, and in particular there has been much scholarly debate over the distinction between bishops and presbyters in second-century Christianity. Justin Martyr, one of the second-century apologists, gives us detailed accounts of church worship, as the Christians met together for that purpose. It seems that in the second century the following features belonged to Christian worship: preaching the Word, standing for prayer, singing or chanting the psalms (in responsive manner, solo, or full congregational), weekly communion. According to Nick Needham, 'no musical instruments accompanied the chanting and singing; Christians did not use instruments in their worship in the 2nd century, or indeed for many centuries afterwards. The early church looked on musical instruments as being part of Jewish or pagan worship, but not part of the apostolic tradition of Christian worship'.[20]

- *They show us some of the problems facing the church in the era after the apostles.* Some of the writings were written in polemical contexts; that is, problems had arisen in the church and these had to be dealt with. There were problems of false doctrine and of persecution; there were also localised problems. No church is free from these.

- *They show us the continuing of the Gospel tradition in the era after the apostles.* The writings of the apostolic fathers show us that the elements of New Testament doctrine and of the gospel were faithfully preserved in the church. This is the meaning of *tradition* – the handed-down doctrine. For example, we find a high Christology in the apostolic fathers. The deity of Christ was not in doubt in the second century. The church had more problems with the humanity than with the deity of Jesus Christ. We find an emphasis on the importance of the cross, of faith, of justification by grace, of confession of Christ. It does not require apostles (or even apostolic succession) to ensure that the truth of the gospel is preserved. Christ will preserve his Word through his people.

Second-century heresies

The need for a clear statement of the Christian gospel and the Christian faith became evident as the second century proceeded. It was not enough simply to rehearse the facts of the life of Christ and the statements of the Lord and the apostles. This was an age of many religions, and the Christian faith was competing in the market-place of ideas. As the gospel was preached and as the churches grew, so also the need grew for a defence of the gospel against the heresies which were current.

Before looking at some of these, it is necessary to define two words which will recur in any study of church history:

First, there is the word *heresy* itself. The word comes from the Greek word *hairesis*, a choice. It came to be applied to the choice of philosophical or theological positions which were not in accordance with the Word of God. The history of the church is peppered with accusations of heresy and the identification of heretics. The following points should guide us on this particular subject:

- Not all error is heresy.[21] It is possible to have an error in our formulation and yet not be heretical.

- Heresies have grown within the church. This fact was prophesied by Jesus and the apostles. Jesus said in Matthew 7:15: 'Beware of false prophets...'; Paul warned that after his departure 'grievous wolves would enter in... also of your own selves shall men arise, speaking perverse things, to draw away disciples after them, therefore watch, and remember...' (Acts 20:29-30).

- Heresy often rides on the back of truth. Doctrinal error is in many cases not an obvious contradiction of truth. In most cases what makes it appealing is how plausible and biblical it so often sounds.

- All heresy, under the sovereign hand of God, has served the cause of truth. How can that be if heresy is a perversion of the truth? Because it has often happened that the presence of error has forced the church to define precisely her creeds and confessions and her systems of truth-belief. It was the heresies of these early centuries which led to the calling of church councils which gave us the credal formulations upon which our orthodoxy is built.

A second word which we need to know is the word *apologetic* (and related words like 'apologist'). This word has nothing to do with being sorry for something. An apologetic is simply a defence. It is the word Peter uses in 1 Peter 3:15 where he urges Christians to be ready to give a *reason* for the hope that is in them. Apologetics is the theological discipline concerned with defending the faith against error and heresy. From the beginning there were apologists in the church, skilled in analysing the streams of thought current at the time and able to present a validly argued rationale for Christan faith.

The next stage is to define some of the second-century heresies and the apologists who answered them.

(1) Gnosticism

Until 1945, with the discovery of some texts in Nag Hammadi in Egypt, most of our knowledge of Gnosticism came from those who opposed it. But the discovery of these writings (52 manuscripts in 12 volumes) from the Gnostics themselves helps us to understand the movement on its own terms. 'Gnosticism' comes from the Greek word *gnosis*, which means *knowledge*. Although there seems to have been a wide variety within Gnosticism itself, the basic idea of the movement was that everything material was evil, and only what could be known by pure spirit was good. Those who knew God in this way could rise above matter and could have enlightenment and salvation.

Gnosticism, although not Christian in origin, appealed to certain aspects of Christian teaching. Had not the apostles taught that Christ saved us from the present *evil world*, and that to *know* God is eternal life? But Gnosticism ignored the fact that matter in and of itself is not evil, and that it is only through Christ that we can have knowledge of God. In Gnosticism, Christ saves by imparting revelation, not by dying on the cross. One view holds that Simon Magus, of whom we read in Acts 8, was the father of Gnosticism.

(2) Docetism

This comes from the Greek word *dokein*, to seem or to appear to be something. This was related to the Gnostic heresy, but was particularly a christological heresy – a heresy centring around the person of Christ. Docetism taught that Christ was not truly human. If all material substance is evil, our physical bodies are evil. Therefore, in the incarnation, Christ took something evil when he took human nature. Clearly this could not be the case. The Docetists got round this problem by teaching that Christ only appeared to be human.

This view rode on the back of the high Christology of the apostolic church. The church of the New Testament and of the second century believed and taught the deity of Jesus Christ. He was acknowleged and confessed as God manifest in the flesh. In his first epistle, probably written between 80 and 85, John is aware of the presence of another teaching. In 1 John 4:3 the apostle says that 'every spirit that does not confess that Jesus Christ is come in the flesh is not from God; and that is that spirit of antichrist, of which you have heard that it should come; and even now already it is in the world'. There is a clear awareness of the idea current among some that Jesus was not truly human. The heresy appeared in various forms, all presenting a Christ other than the God-man of the Gospels.

(3) Montanism

Montanism flourished around the middle of the second century. Montanus was not long a convert to the Christian faith in Mysia when he claimed to be in receipt of special prophecies and revelations from God. He believed that his ecstatic experiences showed that God had specially chosen him to be a communicator of God's revelation. Many believers attached themselves to him. These included several women, which occasioned the charge of loose morals among Montanists. The evidence for this is not conclusive, however.

Williston Walker, the church historian, suggests that Montanism developed because 'the early hope of the speedy return of Christ was growing dim'.[22] Since there was an apparent failure of the Christian hope, something new was required. Walker also suggests that consciousness of the work of the Holy Spirit in the church was also failing. Some prominent churchmen, such as Tertullian of Carthage became Montanists, attracted by various aspects of the movement.

The Montanist movement undermined the final authority of God's revelation in Scripture. It offered new visions, new revelations and new experiences. It has parallels in the growth of modern pentecostalism and the charismatic movement.

The second-century apologists and their arguments for Christianity
Our knowledge of those who defended the Christian faith against these views depends largely on the writings which have survived from antiquity. There may have been more. Quadratus was the bishop or

presbyter of Athens at the beginning of the second century. He addressed the emperor Hadrian, contrasting Christian and pagan worship. One of the most famous apologists was Justin Martyr, who ministered in Ephesus and Rome. He had been trained in Greek philosophy and was able to make a clear, logical defence of Christianity. But both William Cunningham and Cornelius Van Til argue that the defect in Justin's work is his pre-occupation with Greek philosophy. Theophilus of Antioch wrote in defence of Christianity against the pagan philosophers, and Tatian, a pupil of Justin, wrote a famous work called the *Diatessaron*, which was the first attempt to harmonise the Gospel records.

The apologists had no easy task. Louis Berkhof says that

> their task assumed a threefold character – defensive, offensive and constructive. They defended Christianity by showing that there was no evidence for the charges brought against its adherents...and that the character and lives of those who professed the Christian faith were marked by moral purity.... They charged the Jews with...legalism ...they exposed the unworthy, absurd and immoral character of the heathen [pagan] religion...they also felt it incumbent on them to establish the character of Christianity as a positive revelation of God.[23]

These thinkers and writers laid the foundation for much subsequent theological enquiry. They argued that all truth found in pagan philosophers anticipated Christianity, that the miracles of Christ and the apostles proved the truth of Christianity, and that only the Christian philosophy/revelation could satisfy the deepest needs of men.

Conclusion

The second century was a century of adaptation and of consolidation. The primary truths of Christianity continued to be preached, but there was required a constant adaptation and defence of the Christian message in the light of the needs of the hour, and the pressures brought to bear on the Christian church. Persecutions continued, since the Roman Empire could not easily swallow the new religion. Many were martyred for the faith. But the blood of the martyrs proved to be the seed of the church, and facing many difficulties and problems, the church maintained its witness to the finished work of Christ and the superiority of his religious movement.

The Third Century – Consolidation

Important dates

235-38	Persecution under the emperor Maximinus
254	Death of Origen
258	Martyrdom of Cyprian

As the work of the church progressed, one of the pressing needs of the Christian community was to establish the rule of faith, or the creed; there was a need for a clear statement of what the church believed. From about 200, we find the emergence of a statement of belief common to many patristic writers, which came to be known eventually as the Apostles' Creed. It was not determined by a single council or Assembly, but evolved from the earliest writings that we have from the third century until it emerged in its final form around 750.

The Apostles' Creed is still used as a confession of faith in many churches. It is sometimes referred to as the Old Roman creed:

I believe in God the Father Almighty, Creator of Heaven and earth, and in Jesus Christ His only Son, our Lord, who was born of the virgin Mary, suffered under Pontius Pilate, was crucified, died and was buried. [He descended into hell]. On the third day he rose again. He ascended into heaven and is seated at the right hand of God the Father Almighty, from where He will come again to judge the living and the dead. I believe in the Holy Spirit, the holy Catholic Church, the forgiveness of sins, the resurrection of the dead and the life everlasting.[24]

We should note two points about the Apostles' Creed:

- the creed emerged largely as a response to the Gnostic heresy. The presence of error and the need for a strong defence of the gospel in the early church necessitated a clear formulation of

Christian and evangelical belief. In this way, the false doctrine was overruled by God and served the cause of Christ by making the church produce a clear statement of faith.

- The acceptance by the Western Church of the creed has been paralleled by controversy over the inclusion of the phrase 'He descended into hell'. There are, I think, sound biblical and theological reasons for the rejection of this phrase; but there are also historical reasons for regarding it as not an authentic part of the creed as originally formulated. In the writings of the church fathers, the earliest manuscript which contains this formulation appears in the fifth century.[25]

The importance of creeds

Since the third century introduces us to the idea of creeds, it is important that we take time to ask whether creeds and confessions serve any useful purpose. After all, if we believe in the sufficiency and authority of Scripture, what do we need creeds for? Is it not enough to say that we believe the Bible to be true? Do we need statements of doctrine in addition?

The true church has always insisted on the supremacy of Scripture. Nothing in Scripture is negotiable; we cannot say that it is true in some of its parts but not in others, and we must accept its authority in every area of life. But the moment we say 'I believe ...' on the basis of what we read in Scripture, we are making a credal statement. The church commits itself to its creeds and confessions to clarify what it believes the Scriptures to teach. But it always reserves to itself the necessary right to change its confession or creed if it can be demonstrated that the particular creed in question does not accord with Scripture.

A catholic church

As the third century began, the picture of the church continues to blossom and flourish. Historians now talk about the 'catholic' church. Catholic is a beautiful word; it simply means 'universal'. It gives a picture of the church spreading over the world, with people in different parts and different places sharing a common creed and a common interest, engaged in the worship of Jesus and seeking to serve the King of Kings and the Lord of Lords.

Historians often talk about the Christian leaders of the third century as the early catholic fathers. In a sense we are still in the age of the apostolic fathers, but when historians talk about the catholic fathers they refer to a more geographically spread-out group of church leaders.

One of the most famous of these was Irenaeus of Gaul (c.140-202), whose influence would extend into the late second and early third century. He was taught by Polycarp of Smyrna (c.70-155), who had been a disciple of John the apostle. So with Irenaeus there was still a strong link with the apostolic era. In 177 he was at Lyons in Gaul (France), but he escaped a terrible persecution of the church there and became a presbyter or bishop of the church at Lyons. His chief work was entitled *Against Heresies*. He had a strong belief in the imminent return of Christ. One of his writings contrasts the disobedience of Eve with the obedience of Mary, and the prominence he gave to Mary was a weak point in his teaching. But Irenaeus of Gaul features prominently in this period, and he accepted the authority of the New Testament as well as of the Old, giving them canonical status as sacred history.

We also find a growing centre of importance at Rome, the centre of the Roman Empire. One of the prominent names there in the third century is that of Hippolytus (c.170-235) who wrote many commentaries on the Bible, although he favoured allegory as the key to interpreting Scripture. But he seems to have been involved in controversy with various bishops of Rome and the church there does not appear to have been united at this time.

The schools of North Africa: (1) Alexandria

The gospel continued to spread in the years after the apostles. Interestingly, however, it is the men from North Africa that are prominent in the history of this period. We do not know when the gospel came to North Africa, but at the end of the second century, there emerges a strong church in Africa, with two important centres of Christian learning.

The first of these was Alexandria, the Egyptian city called after Alexander the Great. It has been described as 'the second city of the ancient world, surpassed only by Rome, and later by Constantinople'.[26] It was important as far back as 200 BC, when the Septuagint, the

Greek translation of the Old Testament, was translated there. Alexandria was a city of learning. It boasted one of the best libraries and one of the best museums of the ancient world. It is interesting that in Acts 18:24ff we meet Apollos, who was a Jew born at Alexandria, 'an eloquent man and mighty in the Scriptures.' So there is New Testament evidence for the city of Alexandria as a centre of excellence.

Alexandrian Christianity was a powerful force in this seat of learning, and some brilliant teachers were raised up by God to defend and promote the faith. The problem was that in some cases the theology of the apostles came under the influence of Alexandrian – Greek – philosophy. But it is at Alexandria that we come across some of the most brilliant and advanced of the catholic church fathers.

The first was Clement (c.150-215), who had been trained in a school in Alexandria by a converted philosopher, Pantaenus. Clement was converted in his adult years, having trained in philosophy, and he then succeeded Pantaenus as the head of the catechetical school there. Clement was also a presbyter in the church in Alexandria. His three main works were his *Exhortation to the Greeks* (or 'Heathen'), a defence of Christianity; his *Instructor* (or Pedagogue) which was a treatise on Christian conduct, and his *Stromata* (or Miscellanies), a collection of his thoughts on religion. Clement believed that Christ was the source of all true philosophy, as the Logos, or the Word. The weakness in Clement's thought was the high place he gave to philosophy. He said that as the law was the schoolmaster to bring the Hebrews to Christ, philosophy was the schoolmaster to bring the Greeks to Christ.

Clement's pupil was to outshine his teacher as a Christian leader of the third century. His name was Origen (c.184-254) and he succeeded Clement as head of the catechetical school in Alexandria. Origen's father had been a martyr for the faith, and he himself had grown up familiar with the Scriptures. He lived a very ascetic life, concentrating on the study of the Bible and the teaching of his students. He visited Greece and Palestine around 230, and was imprisoned, tortured and put to death at the hands of the Romans.

Of Origen one historian has written that 'no man of purer spirit or nobler aims ornaments the history of the ancient church'.[27] He wrote the first great systematic theology of the church, and a work *Against Celsus*, defending the Christian faith against a pagan critic. He distinguished between the literal and the spiritual sense of Scripture (the allegorical method). To these he added the moral sense, that is, the meaning of the Scripture for life and conduct. On the one hand, this affirmed the literal meaning of the Bible, and highlighted that the Bible is a spiritual book and a practical book. The difficulty is that allegory allowed fanciful interpretations in which the spiritual meaning was divorced from the literal and historical sense, an error into which more than one minister has fallen! A.M. Renwick says of him that 'in the field of speculation, Origen's imagination ran riot'.[28] But the structure of Origen's theology and of his Christology was a great achievement and benefit for the church.

The schools of North Africa: (2) Carthage

The other centre of Christianity in third-century North Africa was Carthage. One of the most influential theologians of Carthage was Tertullian (c.155-220), the son of a Roman army officer who trained in law and was converted in middle age. Although he embraced Montanism, he was nonetheless an important theologian and apologist for the faith. He has been called the father of Latin theology because he was one of the first church writers to use Latin.

Unlike the Alexandrians, Tertullian did not engage in speculation; as a law-man, his thinking was ordered and logical. His doctrines were carefully thought out and defined. Christianity means for Tertullian knowledge of God. It is a new law, and the church is our means to discovering the knowledge of God's being and God's nature. He had a doctrine of original sin and salvation based on grace. Tertullian wrote a great deal, and much of what he wrote has survived. Some of what he wrote would lay the foundation for Papal despotism in later years; he argued, for example, that the church should have nothing whatsoever to do with heretics and that tradition was of equal importance to Scripture. We know that these were wrong views; what is surprising is not that in the third century there were errors in the thinking of some believers, but that even two hundred years after Christ the truth of the gospel was still preserved. The influence of the Latin writings of Tertullian is seen in the fact that many theological terms like 'Trinity', 'substance', and 'sacrament', which are not Bible words, are found in his writings and came to be used by the western church in its theological formulations.

Tertullian was followed by Cyprian (c.200-58), who was converted to Christ in 245. He became bishop of Carthage in 247. He was a man of wealth and learning, who looked after the church in Carthage well and also developed some of the themes in Tertullian. In particular, Cyprian taught the supremacy and authority of the episcopal succession, which brought an unwarranted distinction into the church between the office-bearers of the church (and possibly between the office-bearers and the people). He taught that Peter was the original bishop, and Rome the chief church. But again, in spite of these errors, and amid much persecution, Cyprian encouraged Christians to be strong.

Persecutions of the third century

Although there were periods of peace, the third century continued to see the Roman Empire attack and persecute the Christian church. From 202-11, under the Emperor Septimius Severus, conversion to Christianity was forbidden. In 235 and 236, under Maximinus, many Christian clergy were executed. Between 249 and 251 under Decius, there was an empire-wide persecution of believers, and a return to paganism was required of Christians. From 257 to 260 under Valerian, Christians were not allowed to assemble, and their property in many cases was confiscated.

During the periods of quiet and of peace, many rich families were converted and embraced the faith. This allowed the gospel to flourish and the church to grow throughout the empire. But Decius and Valerian shook the church with their opposition and their persecution. Many Christians remained faithful, but many lapsed and denied the faith.

This had two consequences. First, the courage of many Christians under persecution and threat of death gave great impetus and encouragement to their fellow-believers. To watch men and women holding on to their faith even under threat of death both convinced unbelievers of the truth of the Christian religion, and enabled believers to be strong in the grace of the Lord Jesus Christ.

At the same time, these persecutions led to divisions within the church. Church leaders were divided over the question of what ought to be done with someone who had lapsed and denied the faith but then wanted to return to the church? Some said that the church should accept their repentance and allow them back in; others disagreed.

Other names

At the end of the third century there were some further men who came to prominence as theologians and teachers, such as Dionysius of Alexandria, a pupil of Origen, who continued much of his master's method and viewpoint. Firmilian of Caesarea in Cappadocia was a friend of Origen, who was to have great influence over the Eastern Church. Gregory Thaumaturgos ('wonder-worker'), another pupil of Origen was an effective evangelist in Northern Asia Minor (Turkey).

So God continued to raise men whose influence spread far and wide, and whose teaching shaped the thinking of men so that the gospel continued to be propounded, defended and promoted even in the darkest periods.

Controversies over the doctrine of the Trinity

One theological controversy which had its roots in the third century was to have far-reaching consequences in later years. As we have already noted, the early church gladly acknowledged and confessed the deity of Christ; the Docetics had trouble with his humanity. A more refined version of this heresy developed in Monarchianism (it was Tertullian who gave this name to this particular theology).

Monarchianism begins with the fact that there is only one, sovereign God. He is the *monarch*. Against the polytheism of pagan religion, this was a strong element of the church's confession.

With its confession that Jesus is God, the Monarchians had to get round the fact that only one God was confessed, and yet the Bible taught a plurality with respect to God. How does the doctrine of God's *unity* and *oneness* relate to the fact, for example, that the Father is called God and that Jesus is also called God? In the third century, Monarchianism was an attempt to safeguard both the unity of God and the deity of Christ.

This teaching took two forms. One is known as *dynamic* Monarchianism, which argued that Jesus, although equal with God and of the same substance as God, was not a Person of the Godhead. Paul of Samosata, bishop of Antioch in the late third century, argued that Jesus was a man who was penetrated and infused with divine power to the extent that 'out of man he became God'. The deity of Jesus was a result, therefore, of the deification of Jesus. On this view, Jesus is God because he *became* God.

The other form of this heresy is known as *modalistic* Monarchianism, which was more influential. It argued that the one God manifested himself in different modes or ways, sometimes as Father, sometimes as Son, and sometimes as Holy Spirit. In this formulation, one Person, God, reveals himself in three different modes. Modalistic Monarchianism defended the true divinity of Jesus, but nonetheless had serious flaws.

In the Western Church, modalistic Monarchianism was known as *Patripassianism* (the Father suffering). The argument was that if the one God (=one Person) sometimes manifests himself as Father, sometimes as Son, then the same Person who is the Father also suffered on the cross. Patripassianism is the doctrine that the Father suffered in and with Jesus Christ. This doctrine was called *Sabellianism* in the East, after its famous teacher. Sabellius held firmly to the unity of God, but used the word 'person' in its original sense of an 'actor', and argued that the Persons of the Godhead represent the one God and Father 'acting' in different ways.

Strictly speaking, this teaching grew out of difficulties over Christology, but became a trinitarian controversy, which led to the first major church council in the early fourth century.

This highlights the importance of knowing church history. These errors occur in different forms in modern theology, and can creep in whenever the attempt is made to define orthodox theology. We maintain the unity of God, but we also maintain the triunity of God, the oneness and the more-than-oneness of the Divine Being. These biblical doctrines are not easy to rationalise, although they are not irrational. In combating an error on one side, it was – and is – all too possible to swing then to the other extreme.

Christianity in Britain
Interestingly, there are references in both Tertullian and Origen to

Christianity in Britain in the third century. Some inscriptions at York also testify to a Christian presence in Britain in the third century. However, we know very little about the form this presence took, or the extent of Christian influence in Britain at this time.

Conclusion
Williston Walker summarises the situation at the end of the third century like this:

> By 300 Christianity was effectively represented in all parts of the empire. Its distribution was very unequal, but it was influential in the central provinces of political importance, in Asia Minor, Macedonia, Syria, Egypt, northern Africa, central Italy, southern Gaul and Spain. Nor was its upward progress in the social scale less significant. During this period it won many officers of government and imperial servants. Most important of all, it now began to penetrate the army on a considerable scale ...[29]

Creeds and Councils

NICAEA	325	Called by Emperor Constantine; declared the Son to be of the same substance (*homoousios*) with the Father. Condemned Arius. Drafted the Nicene creed.
CONSTANTINOPLE	381	Produced revised Nicene creed. Affirmed deity of the Holy Spirit. Condemned Apollinarianism (a doctrine that denied the true humanity of Christ.
EPHESUS	431	Condemned Nestorianism (which denied the uni-Personality of Christ).Condemned Pelagius (who taught that man is born good and capable of saving himself).
CHALCEDON	451	Declared Christ's two natures were unchanged and undivided; affirmed the unity of Christ's person. Condemned Eutychianism (which denied the true humanity of Christ).
CONSTANTINOPLE	680	Condemned monothelitism (the teaching that Christ had only one (divine) will.
NICAEA	787	Declared that it was lawful to venerate images.

The Fourth Century – Controversy

Important dates

312	Conversion of Constantine
323	Building of St Peter's, Rome, begins
325	Council of Nicaea
325-81	Controversy over Arianism
381	Council of Constantinople
396	Augustine becomes Bishop of Hippo

One of the fiercest of the Roman persecutions against the Christian church was under the emperor Diocletian, who assumed power in 284 and was emperor at the turn of the century. It is alleged that more Christians died during the persecution of Diocletian than during any other period; but because Christianity had grown and the number of believers had spread, the church survived wonderfully. Diocletian abdicated in 305.

After his father's short period as emperor, Constantine (c.273-337) became emperor in 306. He was engaged in battle at the Milvian Bridge in 312, against one of his rivals. By this time the Roman Empire itself was going through a period of political uncertainty and upheaval, with power blocks in the East and in the West under two rival emperors. It was against one of these rivals that Constantine marched in 312. Eusebius, the fourth-century church historian, tells us that on the eve of the battle Constantine had a vision of the cross shining in the sky, and the words *in hoc signo, vince* – 'in this sign conquer!' emblazoned on the cross. Constantine adopted a new emblem on his shield – the sign of the cross made of the first two letters of Christ's name. This so-called Chi-Rho symbol became one of the earliest symbols of Christianity.

The conversion of Constantine marked a new and significant point in the history of the church. It had several effects.

First, it relaxed the persecution against the believers. Constantine from the beginning of his imperial reign had been willing to tolerate Christianity, but after his conversion he made this toleration a requirement of law. Following the Edict of Milan enacted in 313, confiscated property was to be restored to the Christians, and all religious restrictions were removed.

Second, it gave the gospel a new prominence and began to discriminate against paganism. Historians are divided over the extent to which Constantine's conversion affected Christianity. Some argue that Christianity was given official recognition as the state religion; others say that Constantine simply opened the way for a greater toleration of Christianity. Whatever the facts of the situation are, it is true that as a result of Constantine's conversion, the recognition of Christianity gave the church a public prominence it had not had before. Conversely, paganism, in many of its forms, began to be marginalised, although many throughout the Empire adhered to pagan rites and rituals.

Third, it changed the relationship between the church and the state. The new bond that was forged between the empire and the church laid the foundation for many later controversies which would divide churches – the question of the relationship which ought to be between church and state. Some Christians and historians have argued that any church-state relationship is disastrous; others believe that because of the sovereignty of Christ over both church *and* state there must be some relationship between them. Historians like Owen Chadwick can talk about the 'Christian Empire' which emerged as a result of Constantine's policies. At one level that was good; but other historians, like Williston Walker, argue that 'in winning its freedom from its enemies, [the church] had come largely under the control of the occupant of the Roman imperial throne. A fateful union with the state had begun'.[30] Another historian has said that 'in the centuries that followed, the cross and the sword were to be involved in a constant and sometimes violent battle of will'.[31]

Fourth, it had the effect of formalising the practice of Christianity. The early Christians were serious about their faith. Had they not been, they would not have been as steadfast and as faithful under opposition and persecution. But there does not appear to have been much formalisation of church rite and practice until the time of

Constantine. Not humble by nature, Constantine was always dressed in rich finery; at one point he presented the Bishop of Jerusalem with clerical vestments, adorned and splendid, to rival those of the pagan priests. This was one of the first instances of vestments of a special kind to be used by the clergy.

This, in turn, led to increased clericalism in the church. The church organisation of the second and third centuries had been very simple; but following Constantine's wishes, gradually church councils assumed greater power, and gave bishops increased power and authority. There was a clear division – an unbiblical division – between clergy and laity, between ministers and people.

So the conversion of Constantine was a great blessing for himself personally, but a mixed blessing for the religion of Jesus Christ. We should learn the lesson of how much good the conversion of our statesmen and political leaders can do, but also how we need to fashion and model our Christianity on the dictates of Christ in his word, and not on the political correctness of this world. The Christian church has to live in the shadow of the cross, not the shadow of the sword.

The Council of Nicaea

One of the high marks of the fourth century was the calling of the Council of Nicaea in 325. This was called by Constantine to deal with a doctrinal controversy. We have already noted the way in which Monarchianism grew in the church, in different forms, as a way of safeguarding both the unity of God and the deity of Jesus Christ. This trinitarian controversy became more complex and developed into the fourth century.

It is known as the Arian Controversy after Arius (c. 256-336), a presbyter from Alexandria. His starting-point, and the dominant note of his theology, was the Monarchian position of the oneness and absolute sovereignty of God. Arius began to teach that the Son of God must therefore be a lesser, created being; the greatest of all God's creation, but a creature nonetheless. In Arius' view, 'There was when he (the Son) was not.' Arius believed that as the Father the Supreme Being had brought the Son into being as the one through whom the world would be made. Thus, the Supreme Being was able to maintain a suitable distance from the material world.

Arius was first disciplined by his bishop, Alexander, who defended the true divinity of Christ. But Alexander did not have the same clear theological insight as the man who succeeded him in 328 as bishop of Alexandria – Athanasius. Athanasius insisted on formulating his Christology in terms of the unity of God and in terms of a doctrine of trinity that would not undermine that unity. Athanasius said that the divine essence, the being of God, was indivisible, while there were distinctions in God in terms of Persons (hypostases). The Son was not created, he argued, but had an independent and underived personal existence. So Athanasius did the church a great service by recognising that it was necessary to speak of the oneness of God while recognising personal distinctions within that oneness.

Constantine called the Council of Nicaea to deal, amongst other things, with this controversy in his empire. Needham says, 'About 300 bishops were present, and an even larger number of presbyters and deacons.'[32] Constantine was present in person and seems to have used his influence to secure as much unanimity as possible. In the event, Arianism was declared heretical, but only two people (Arius and a fellow-presbyter) were found guilty of it. They were deposed and banished.

The Council led to the formulation of the Nicene Creed:

We believe in one God,
the Father the Almighty, maker of heaven and earth, of
all that is, seen and unseen.
We believe in one Lord Jesus Christ, the only Son of
God, eternally begotten of the Father, God from God, light
from light, true God from true God, begotten, not made, of
one Being with the Father.
Through him all things were made. For us men and for
our salvation he came down from heaven; by the power of
the Holy Spirit he became incarnate from the Virgin Mary,
and was made man.
For our sake he was crucified under Pontius Pilate; he
suffered death and was buried. On the third day he rose
again in accordance with the Scriptures; He ascended into
heaven and is seated at the right hand of the Father. He

will come again in glory to judge the living and the dead, and his kingdom will have no end.

We believe in the Holy Spirit, the Lord, the giver of life, who proceeds from the Father (and the Son). With the Father and the Son he is worshipped and glorified. He has spoken through the Prophets.

We believe in one holy, catholic and apostolic Church. We acknowledge one baptism for the forgiveness of sins. We look for the resurrection of the dead, and the life of the world to come. Amen.[33]

In addition, the Council pronounced a series of anathemas against various Arian statements. It bequeathed to the church a framework for the biblical doctrine of the Trinity. The church is committed to the *homo-ousios*, to the fact that Jesus is not simply *like* God, and not simply *from* God, but that he *is* God. The whole debate that led to Nicaea was driven not simply by academic theological concerns, but by concerns over the gospel itself. It was recognised that if Christ were a creature, or some kind of superior being who was simply like God, then he could not be our Saviour. Only the fact that he is of the same essence as God safeguards the Christian faith, the gospel and the life of the church.

At the time when it was convened there was no suggestion that there was anything special about the Council of Nicaea. It was only later it acquired the status of the first ecumenical Council. Moreover, it was only later that its creed acquired special prestige. The immediate effect of the Council was to drive Arianism underground for a generation or so. The issues of the controversy resurfaced in earnest in the 350s, a period marked by frequent councils and a spate of credal statements. At this stage there were three main groups. First there were the radical Arians led by Aetius and Eunomius. They claimed the Son was *hetero-ousios*, of a *different* substance to the Father. They were opposed by a group who wanted greater authority for the Nicene Creed and its key word *homo-ousios*. Athanasius was the main leader of this group. Finally, there was a middle party who wished to describe the Son as *homoio-ousios*, of a similar substance to the Father. They disliked the Nicene formulation because they believed it to be tainted with Sabellianism.

Most of the creeds which were published in the 350s (with one exception) were not blatant Arian statements. They were designed as accommodating declarations which would rule out as few as possible. As such, they obtained imperial support. Over time, however, it became clear that these creeds had allowed Arianising clerics to assume positions of power within the church and in this way spread their doctrines. The result was that the Nicene Creed acquired the reputation of being a sure bulwark against Arianism; its supposed Sabellian tendencies were dismissed. Among those who came to champion the Nicene doctrine were a younger group of men – Basil of Caesarea, Gregory Nazianzus and Gregory of Nyssa, sometimes known as the Three Cappadocians.

The Council of Constantinople

The second ecumenical council was held in Constantinople in 381. As with the Council of Nicaea, it was only graced with this title some time later. This Council seems to have reaffirmed the Nicene Creed and made a few additions to it. Whereas the original Nicene Creed had stated simply 'we believe in the Holy Spirit', this was now deemed inadequate. Different views had emerged regarding the Holy Spirit. If Nicaea had done anything, it had upset the views of those who were inclined to think of the Godhead as a hierarchy with the Father at the top, the Son in the middle and the Spirit taking up third place. But when Nicaea affirmed the co-equality and unisubstantiality of the Father and the Son, this seemed to leave the Holy Spirit tagged on to the other two persons, subordinate to both the Father and the Son.

The Council of Constantinople expanded the clause dealing with the Holy Spirit. While these additions did not assert in as many words that the Spirit is God, they implied that. One of these additions was destined to provoke controversy in the future, for the extended Nicene Creed affirmed that the Holy Spirit proceeded from the Father. This was to be the position maintained in the Eastern Church even after the Western Church moved, as we shall see, to a biblical doctrine of double procession, eventually confessing that the Holy Spirit proceeds from the Father 'and from the Son'.

The Council was anxious to avoid the charge of innovation in its doctrinal statement. Hence its caution over what it said about the Holy Spirit. But debates about the status of the Spirit continued elsewhere. It became common in the eastern churches to regard the Father as somehow the originator of the deity of the Son and of the Spirit, the so-called *fons deitatis*, the fount of divinity. But this did not seem naturally to arise from the texts of Scripture. Gregory Nazianzus came closer to the biblical position when he argued for a distinction between *generation* as regards the Son and *procession* as regards the Spirit. But he still maintained that it was from the Father alone that the Spirit proceeded.

The Council of Constantinople also issued an important ruling that 'the Bishop of Constantinople shall have the Primacy of honour after the bishop of Rome, because Constantinople is new Rome'.[34] Constantinople had emerged as the imperial capital of the Greek-speaking East, while Rome remained the imperial centre in the Latin-speaking West. The church was divided into *sees* (or areas governed by a bishop), roughly corresponding to the administrative units of the Roman Empire. Because of the dominance of Rome, the bishop there was given the name *papa* ('father') from which the term 'pope' is derived. It was claimed that Peter was the first bishop, or pope, of Rome. By contrast, Constantinople had no apostolic tradition to give it prominence, so some suggested that Andrew, Peter's brother, had founded the diocese there. But given its political importance, it was inevitable that Constantinople should begin to dominate ecclesiastically in the East.

This tendency became even more pronounced after 395, when the Roman Empire formally divided into two. Two distinct church traditions were emerging. In the East there was the Greek Orthodox Church, centred at Constantinople, and the Latin Roman Catholic Church in the West, centred at Rome. And whatever our view of either the Orthodox Church or the Roman Catholic Church, it was mainly in these streams of religious tradition that the truth was preserved from the fourth century through the Middle Ages until the Reformation era gave birth to biblical Protestantism.

Great leaders of the fourth century

The emperor Constantine died in 337, after having exerted his own particular influence on the direction of the church for some twenty-five years since his conversion. The empire was divided between his sons, so that East and West were under different emperors. This did not help to heal the divisions in the church caused as a result of continuing controversy and divisions between the Eastern and the Western churches. However, God raised up some great men to lead and guide his people, among whom were the following:

- Eusebius of Caesarea (c.260-340) was the first to specialise in the study of church history. Eusebius had the ear of the emperor, and tried to mediate between the Arians and the anti-Arians in the Nicene controversy. He wrote a history of the church.

- Hilary of Poitiers (d.367) was converted late in life. He wrote on the Trinity, and was a strong opponent of Arianism in the West. In the middle of the fourth century he was appointed bishop of Poitiers.

- Ambrose of Milan (c.337-97) received a good education in Rome, and was trained for a career in the civil service. Around 374 he became governor of a large area of northern Italy. Although he had never been baptized, he was appointed bishop of Milan when the bishopric fell vacant, and he gave up his wealth for the poor, devoting himself to the study of theology. He was an authoritative teacher and a man of humility and grace. One of his sayings illustrates this: 'I will not glory because I am righteous, but I will glory because I am redeemed. I will not glory because I am free from sin, but because my sins are forgiven.'

- John Chrysostom (c.347-407) lived and ministered during the last years of the fourth century in Antioch and Constantinople. He was one of the great preachers of the early church, and because his preaching was so anointed of God he was nicknamed *chrysostom*, 'golden-mouthed'. His sermons were exegetically based and full of practical and social application.

Development of Rome

It was largely during the fourth century that Rome became a centre of strategic importance for the church. The building of St Peter's began around 323, and in 343 a church council, the Council of Sardica, recognised the jurisdiction of Rome. Coupled with this was the development of the monastic life, in which certain believers isolated themselves from the world, and lived in monasteries where they followed ascetic practices and sought absolute devotion to God. Alongside this there developed the rise of nunneries for women. There was also an insistence on the celibacy of bishops. This ascendancy of Rome and the development of separate religious orders laid the foundation for the Roman Catholicism with which we are so familiar today. In the fourth century the concept of the papacy was gradually entrenched in the thinking of the church.

It was in the monastic system of the fourth century that we find Jerome (c.345-420), the great translator of the Bible into Latin, doing his work. He was a very educated man, who knew both Greek and Hebrew. At one stage in his life he was the secretary of Damasus, bishop of Rome, and his Latin Bible, the Vulgate, was to become the official Bible of the Roman Catholic Church.

One of the most important figures in late fourth-century church history is Augustine, Bishop of Hippo (354-430), and we will be returning to him next century, since most of his creative and important work was done at the beginning of the fifth century. He was born at Tagaste in North Africa; his parents became Christians, and in his *Confessions* he talks movingly of the influence of his pious mother, Monica. He was converted in 386, after having studied philosophy and rhetoric. He was an ardent admirer of the philosophy of Plato, and it is hard to find any of his larger writings which does not have a marked Platonist influence.

Augustine became the bishop of Hippo in 396, and by the end of the fourth century he had already written strong material against various errors and heresies in the church. He gave himself to the study of the Scriptures and emphasised the importance of the Old Testament, and also of the catholicity of the church. It was at this time that he abandoned his earlier optimistic belief in human nature – becoming a minister confirmed for him the doctrine of total depravity!

During the years 397 to 401 Augustine wrote his *Confessions*, in which he testified to the great grace of God in his life. He became one of the greatest Latin fathers of the church, and wrote widely on Christian doctrine and exegesis. Gerald Bray says of him that he 'raised the standard of Christian learning immeasurably. No ancient writer has left us more material, and few have so stamped their own personality on it. Augustine's was a very human genius which has never ceased to appeal to Christians of every nation, age and culture.'[35]

One of his polemics in the fourth century was against Donatism, a view which had been current in the church since about 311, which said that clergymen who had lapsed under persecution were unworthy of being readmitted into the church and were invalidated from conferring the sacraments. Behind this view was a view of the church as an institution whose purity was not to be compromised by the readmission of unfaithful ministers. Augustine's reply to the Donatists was based on the twofold argument that a pure church could not be found in this world, and that 'the unworthiness of the minister did not affect the validity of the sacrament whose minister was Christ'.[36]

Augustine, however, is a curious mix. On the one hand he held a very high view of the one catholic church and its sacraments. Outside this church there was no hope of salvation, even among those groups whom we would consider to have had good reason to leave that church. And yet on the other hand he laid the foundation for sound biblical thinking on the doctrines of grace. He is consequently appealed to by Protestants. I am reminded of Rabbi Duncan's statement that 'Augustine was greater on the whole than Calvin.... Calvin was standing on Augustine's shoulders.'[37] But he is also appealed to by Roman Catholics; for example, in an article on early church attitudes to divorce and remarriage, one author has written that 'the teaching of the Roman Catholic Church was based on the formulations of Augustine of Hippo, who regarded marriage as a sacrament'.[38] The Roman Catholic Church also finds warrant for including the Apocrypha in the canon on the basis of Augustine's writings. Augustine's view of the Apocrypha as fully scriptural reflects his high view of the Septuagint which he thought genuinely to be the consensus of seventy translators of the Hebrew into the Greek. Since so many had agreed to publish the Apocrypha along with the other Hebrew Scriptures, their judgment should not be overturned without good reason.

Therefore, although Augustine was a theological giant, his doctrine of the church was flawed. B.B. Warfield suggests that without Augustine no branch of the Christian church could have developed as it has, but that 'the Reformation, inwardly considered, was just the ultimate triumph of Augustine's doctrine of grace over Augustine's doctrine of the Church'.[39]

St Ninian

Another important date for us to recognise is the establishing of a monastery at Whithorn on the Solway Firth as a result of the missionary activity of Ninian (c.360-432). He came from studying in Rome to evangelise Scotland. Although the details of Ninian's life and work are obscure,[40] it is thought he established his monastery in 397, where he was later buried. He and his disciples were to have an important influence in the development of Celtic Christianity.

Conclusion

By the end of the fourth century the church has moved a great deal from its humble beginnings. The simplicity of worship and lifestyle which characterised the early Christians has given way to a complexity of liturgy and ornamentation which has turned the church into a formal institution. It is arguable that the church would never again know the simple and uncomplicated lifestyle of Christ and the early apostles. The seeds had been sown for future controversies over worship and vestments. However, the truth of God continued to be defended and propagated, and it was this that drew disciples after Jesus Christ.

The Fifth Century – Definition

Important dates

416	Teaching of Pelagius condemned
431	Council of Ephesus
451	Council of Chalcedon
476	End of Roman Empire in the West

The beginning of the fifth century is characterised by some of Augustine's most important work and his most prodigious and industrious output. Two of his concerns are especially worth noting.

The City of God
In 410, Rome was captured by a race known as the Visigoths (tribal Germans). Pagans in Rome said that the disaster was the result of Rome having forsaken its traditional gods, and having embraced the God of the Christians. In order to answer this charge, Augustine wrote his *City of God*, which is really a Christian view of world history. The sack of Rome demonstrated that God's interest was not in any earthly city as such, but the church which he was preserving. Beginning with a view of the world as divided into seven ages, corresponding to the creation days, he believed that the church era was the sixth day, prior to the seventh, eternal Sabbath, and is to be identified with the Millennium of Revelation 20. He argued that the church of God was independent of any state or society, and that God was preserving his church in every generation. The work extended to several volumes, and marks Augustine out as one of the great Christian philosophers.

Anti-Pelagian writings
Augustine is probably best remembered for his role in the Pelagian controversy at the turn of the fifth century. Pelagius was a British monk who came to Rome around 383. He was shocked by some of

55

the worldliness and the ritualism he found there, and he was influential in introducing the monastic order into Rome. Augustine himself had given support to the monastic movement.

Pelagius, therefore, was motivated both by a zeal for holiness and a commitment to Christ. But he was unorthodox in his theology, particularly in his view of human nature. These views are what sparked the Pelagian controversy, which focused on the biblical teaching regarding man. It is interesting to note that controversies over the doctrine of God and the doctrine of Christ were soon accompanied by controversies over the doctrine of man (anthropology).

In Pelagius' view, men are born sinless, just as Adam was. This sinlessness, however, is really a kind of neutrality, because it is possible for us to lose it, just as Adam did. Most follow his example, and sin. Their sin is not because of a corrupt nature, but because of free choice. Some are able to remain pure, sinless and perfectly holy (probably through becoming monks) in this life. Grace is not the work of the Holy Spirit, but is equal to man's own abilities and capabilities.

Would that it were so! But neither the Bible nor our human experience agrees with Pelagius. Why do young infants do wrong things if there is no original sin? And what of the Scriptures that make plain that we have been 'conceived in sin and shaped in iniquity'? Augustine was very much influenced by his study of Paul's letter to the Romans and by the wider testimony of the Scriptures which shows that sin is indeed voluntary, but that the human will cannot *but* sin, until it is freed from the domination and lordship of sin by the grace of God. Augustine regarded sin as the absence of that which is good. Had man remained obedient to God, he would have been confirmed in holiness, and would have passed from the condition of being *able not to sin* to being *unable to sin*. Instead, he fell, and passed into the state of being *unable not to sin*. This lays the foundation for the doctrine of total depravity, and the absolute need of grace to work salvation in the sinner.

The theologian Louis Berkhof summarises: 'In view of all this it was perfectly natural that Augustine's deriving everything, free will included, from divine grace, collided with the opposite tendency, as represented in Pelagius.'[41] The two views were completely at variance with one another. Pelagius' views were propagated in Rome from

409 to 411; they were subsequently disseminated in Carthage by his pupil Celestius. Eventually the church, at an important church council in Ephesus in 431, condemned Pelagianism as heresy. There was a halfway movement between the two extremes, called Semi-Pelagianism which sought to co-ordinate the action of the will and the work of grace in the salvation of man, and this was prominent for a time in Gaul (France). The position of the western churches on this issue remained ambivalent up to the time of the Reformation when Luther, Calvin and other Reformation leaders came down firmly on the side of Augustinian teaching.

Two important councils

The Council of Ephesus

The Council of Ephesus was called by the emperor in June 431. It was required in order to ratify a decision taken by Pope Celestine, bishop of Rome, regarding the nature of the Person of Christ. Arianism threatened the orthodox biblical teaching of the Person of Jesus Christ by its insistence that 'there was when he was not' and had been condemned at Nicaea in 325. The Nicene Council thereby affirmed the consubstantiality and co-equality of the Persons of the Godhead, declaring that Jesus was of the same essence as God. The Council of Ephesus was necessary because of debates that subsequently arose regarding the two natures of Christ, and the relationship between the human nature and the divine.

Those who espoused dynamic Monarchianism had denied the deity of Jesus, while the Docetics and the Gnostics had denied his humanity. One of the first attempts to resolve this difficult and complex doctrine was made by Apollinaris, bishop of Laodicea (c.300-390). Although his dates set him in the fourth century, it was his teachings that permeated certain parts of the church at the beginning of the fifth.

Apollinaris represented the school of Alexandria, which we have already seen to have favoured an allegorical approach to Scripture, in place of the literal view held by the school of Antioch. Antioch taught the distinction between the two natures of Jesus, and insiste '
only by maintaining that distinction was it possible to have an atc
grounded in history. This also ensured that the humanity

was not compromised by attributing his divine qualities to his human personality.

The school at Alexandria was more given to speculation and allegory, and began with a strong insistence on the deity of Christ. The tendency was to represent the two natures as running into one another, minimising the distinction as far as possible. Apollinaris taught that man is body and soul, and that in the incarnation the divine word (the Logos) took the place of the soul in Jesus. In this way he sought to safeguard both the deity of Christ and the sinlessness of Christ. The problem was that if the Logos replaced the soul, then Christ had not assumed a total humanity, and could not therefore be a whole Saviour. Partly in order to deal with this false conception of the constitutive elements of our Lord's human nature, the Council of Constantinople in 381 had asserted the integrity of the Lord's human nature – no part of it had been replaced by anything.

Another name that figured prominently in these controversies over the human nature of Christ was Nestorius of Constantinople (c.381-450s). Part of his concern was with Mary's being called *theotokos*, the mother (or bearer) of God. This reflects the high place given to Mary as early as the fifth century. Nestorius argued that Mary should be called *Christotokos* (mother of Christ), and that Christ should be thought of as a man whom the divine Son of God had united to himself. However, Nestorianism also left itself open to the charge that if Mary gave birth to a man who was subsequently assumed into a relationship with the divine Word, then his was not an effective redemption.

Nestorius had a formidable opponent in the person of Cyril of Alexandria, who wanted to keep the doctrine of the two natures, and also that of the unity of the Person of Christ. He was, however, unwilling to apply the term 'nature' to the Lord's humanity, and some appealed to him as an authority for the belief that the incarnation produced a hybrid nature – a divine/human mixture in a single nature. This is called the monophysite ('one nature') heresy.

The Council of Ephesus condemned Nestorianism on the grounds that it so distinguished between the two natures of Christ as to make them two Persons, or two Christs. However, some of Nestorius' supporters formed their own church as a result and carried the gospel into India and Arabia.

The Council of Chalcedon

In order further to clarify the doctrine, as well as to bring stability to the empire, a new emperor called another council to meet in Chalcedon in October 451. It was really the council of Chalcedon that defined for the church the orthodox doctrine of the Person of Christ. The relevant statement from Chalcedon reads as follows:

> *We then, following the holy Fathers, all with one consent, teach men to confess one and the same Son, our Lord Jesus Christ, the same perfect in Godhead and also perfect in manhood; truly God and truly man, of a reasonable soul and body; consubstantial (*homo-ousion*) with the Father according to the Godhead, and consubstantial with us according to the manhood, in all things like unto us, without sin; begotten before all ages of the Father according to the Godhead, and in these latter days for us and for our salvation born of the Virgin Mary, the Mother of God (*Theotokos*) according to the manhood; one and the same Christ, Son, Lord, Only-begotten, in two natures, inconfusedly, unchangeably, indivisibly, inseparably, the distinction of natures being by no means taken away by the union, but rather the property of each nature being preserved, and concurring in one person (*prosopon*) and one subsistence (*hypostasis*), not parted or divided into two persons, but one and the same Son and only-begotten, God the Word, the Lord Jesus Christ....* [42]

Chalcedon effectively drew a borderline around the church's doctrine of Christ, preserving the unity of Christ's person, the distinction of the two natures, the unity of the two natures without confusion in the one person, and the inseparableness of the two natures in the one person. [43] The Chalcedonian definition is nothing if not 'carefully worded'. [44] In effect, it binds the church by its wording to a specific view of Christ as one who is simultaneously God and man.

It is perhaps a sobering thought that we owe our orthodox belief in this whole area to a council convened by an emperor in the East, and endorsed by Pope Leo the Great! Leo was pope of Rome from 440 to 461, and was to wield a great deal of influence. His influence was such that he was able to persuade the Huns to move out of Italy. But he also persuaded the bishops to acknowledge him as supreme pontiff of the Western Church, whose authority extended back, allegedly, to Peter himself. These claims were treated with great suspicion in the East, but laid the foundation for later claims of papal infallibility. The council, to a large extent, adopted the wording of Leo's *Tome* in its definition. A.M. Renwick says that Leo I 'stands out as the first truly great churchman to appear in Rome since apostolic times'.[45]

Chalcedon did not satisfy everyone, however, and in the churches in the East it caused division. Imperial intrigue and politics became mixed in with the creeds of Alexandria and Antioch – 'the consequence was not peace but confusion'.[46]

The end of the Roman Empire in the West

We have already noted that the city of Rome was besieged by tribal warriors in 410. This was part of an ongoing attack on the Western reaches of the empire by Asian tribesmen. One of the most famous of these was Attila the Hun, who attacked the Germans around mid-fifth century. These tribal victories were to lead to the division of the empire, and to the end of the empire in Western Europe. The Eastern Roman Empire became known as the Byzantine Empire after the prominent city of Byzantium (now renamed Constantinople). The tribes who had taken over Germany had embraced a form of Arianism, preaching the Christian gospel but virtually denying the deity of Jesus Christ, and by the year 476 had effectively destroyed the Roman Empire in the West. The result was that Western Europe was under the dominance of its own kings and tribal leaders rather than under the dominance of the Roman Empire.

One of the most significant occurrences at this time was the conversion of Clovis, who was king of France around 480. He promised God that if God would help him in a battle against the Germanic tribes, he would be baptised. Victory was given him, and he duly embraced the faith. This led to the evangelisation of most of France at the end of the fifth century.

This was, then, a changing world. The supremacy of Rome was

undermined by the barbarian tribes who broke the Western Roman Empire into individual and independent states. The close of the fifth century marks the beginnings of the Dark Ages and the approach of the Middle Ages.

St Patrick

In Great Britain, the fifth century marks an important period in our religious history with the missionary activity of St Patrick (c.386-460). Patrick had been a slave in Ireland for some years at the beginning of the fifth century. When he escaped he spent time in a monastery in France and was ordained in 432. He began a thirty-year period of missionary work and evangelisation in Ireland, which laid the foundations for Celtic Christianity.[47] While we do not have many details for the life of Patrick, it seems clear that he laid the foundation for monastic religion in many parts of Ireland, and many of his disciples were responsible for bringing the gospel to Britain through travel and emigration. The most famous of these was Columba, whose dates bring us to the sixth century, and the next chapter. But by the fifth century there is a marked Christian presence in Ireland, and some of Patrick's prayers have survived, one of the most famous being his 'lorica' or 'breastplate' – a prayer for God's protection and blessing.

In Patrick we see the origins of what has been described as the Celtic Church. Patrick did not bring Christianity to Britain – Pelagius, against whom Augustine wrote much of his material, was a British monk. In fact, following the Pelagian controversy, Germanus, Bishop of Auxerre in France, led a mission to Britain to ensure that the heresy would not take hold. With the collapse of the empire, Roman soldiers were withdrawn from Britain, and this left the nation open to invasion and uprising both within and without. The Picts and the Scots invaded England from the north, while Europeans invaded from the east.

In this context, Christianity took hold and survived in the Celtic fringes and regions of the West. The Celtic church in Ireland was to influence the spread of Christianity in Scotland within the next two centuries. But the separation from the continent of Europe was also a means by which a purer form of the Christian religion was preserved among the peoples of the West.

Developments into the fifth century

By the fifth century, the church as a whole had further moved away from the simplicity which characterised Christ and the early apostles. The place of the pope, the monastic order, and the cult of Mary had all taken root in church life and church practice. Some of the major churches and cathedrals had been built, and relics believed to date back to the time of Christ had been 'discovered' and became objects of veneration and adoration. Different 'orders' of style and liturgy had arisen, with sharp divisions and distinctions between the Greek East and the Latin West. Tradition came to mean something different to what it meant in the New Testament. It came to be revered and regarded as of equal authority to the biblical writings. Priestly celibacy had become a requirement for ministry.

We are only five hundred years removed from Christ – a quarter of the way through our story – but already we can see how the truth was under threat from unbelieving, pagan systems as well as unbiblical religious traditions.

There is a lesson for us in all of this. We are called to the Bible as the only rule which God has given us whereby we can glorify and enjoy him. We must always be jealous to guard the simplicity there is in Christ, and not compromise the truth of the gospel from anything that may jeopardise or threaten it. No age has been without its pitfalls and failings; but we are privileged indeed if we can look back and learn from the history of the church in past ages.

The Sixth Century – Fallout

Important dates

c.540	Benedict write his 'Rule'
563	Columba in Iona
590	Gregory becomes Pope
596	Augustine lands in Kent to convert the British

The aftermath of Chalcedon

The Council of Chalcedon is described by Gerald Bray as marking 'a turning point in the history of theological thought'.[48] It defined the orthodox doctrine of the Person of Christ, and committed the church to the unity of Christ's Person and the distinction between Christ's natures. Further, it taught that these natures were not to be confused with each other, and could not be changed, divided, or separated. It is interesting that the Christology of Chalcedon is expressed mostly in terms of negatives – what Christ is not. Nonetheless, Chalcedon did the church an important service by laying down the borderlines of biblical truth. This did not mean that there would be no more enquiry into the subject. Although the revelation of the Bible is full and complete and closed, we are always able to improve on the formulations of the past. Theological reflection and insight would continue, and we must always build on the Chalcedon formulation.

But there were many who could not accept the Chalcedonian Definition about the Person of the Saviour. The result was that in the late fifth and early sixth centuries, several distinct schools of thought emerged within the church.[49]

One of these was the Monophysite school of thinking. The word 'monophysite', as we have seen, means 'one nature'. The monophysites followed the formulation of Cyril of Alexandria, and rejected Chalcedon. Christ, they said, had one nature, not two. Their argument was that two natures requires two persons; Christ was one

63

person, therefore had one nature. Even within this school of thought, there were moderates and extremists, some who believed that in order to protect the unity of the Lord's Person you need to posit a divine/ human nature, a nature made up of divine and human elements. Others spoke of a mingling of divinity and humanity in the one nature of the Lord. This was the teaching embraced in the Eastern Church in the late fifth and early sixth century. In 553 the Second Council of Constantinople formally embraced this position. Although it did not repudiate Chalcedon or affirm the one nature of Christ, it condemned those who held other views.

In contrast, there was also a 'diophysite' party in the controversy. The diophysites accepted Chalcedon and championed the orthodox doctrine of the two natures. However, there was still a great deal of confusion regarding the relationship of Christ's human nature to his Person, and there was a tendency to drift into a form of Nestorianism, the doctrine that Jesus was a human person.

Monasticism

One of the most important developments of the sixth century was the growth of monasticism. We have already noted that many in the early church felt that the path of virtue and holiness was to be found in complete withdrawal and isolation from the world. This did not begin in the sixth century. But one important date in the history of monasticism is 529, when Benedict of Nursia (c.480-550) and those who had joined him in his hermitic lifestyle moved to Monte Cassino, where they built a purpose-built monastery. By 540 Benedict had formalised the lifestyle of the group with his 'Rule of St Benedict', which established a formal pattern for monastic life which would be emulated in later periods.

Although monastic life was characteristic of the religion of many, there had been little formal order in monasticism up to this point. Some monasteries were lax, others were very strict. Benedict was in a sense 'the great Reformer of Western monasticism'.[50] His rule described what a monastery should be like, and the order and hierarchy which should prevail there. He laid down rules for worship and organisation of both spiritual and temporal duties. Benedict hoped in this way to make the monasteries places primarily for worship, but also for learning, and for the study of theology. His rule was to have a profound influence over the course of Western Church life for many years. Although the system was open to abuse, it nonetheless served the interests of the church and the cause of Christ well, as monks copied and stored the biblical manuscripts, using them in their worship as well as making them part of their study. In this way the Word of God was preserved even within systems that had moved away from that Word.

Gregory the Great

One proof of this is to be found in the influence of Pope Gregory the Great in the sixth century. Gregory was born in Rome in 540 and became a governor of Rome in the 570s. He encouraged the monastic orders, although he did not join one himself. He was a papal ambassador in Constantinople in 579, and was elected pope in 590. He died in 604.

As well as giving a strong lead to the Western Church, Gregory was also an able and efficient statesman, who did much to defend Rome against the Lombards, who were threatening to attack Italy. It was largely through Gregory's influence that the papal office attracted great wealth and grew in power and prestige throughout the empire. He was influential in raising the profile of the papacy in places where there was no marked allegiance of this kind to the bishop of Rome. Gregory was one of the first to preach the doctrine of purgatory and to make a claim for the universal sovereignty and dominion of the Roman See. His influence is felt to this day in the style of reciting the psalms to tunes in the episcopal liturgy, what we know as the Gregorian Chant.

The papacy of Gregory the Great marked the beginning of a distinctive liturgical and ecclesiastical system, upon which much of subsequent Roman Catholicism would be based. The claims of the pope for the universal jurisdiction of Rome, the doctrine of purgatory, praying for the dead and to the saints, adoration of Mary, confession, the priesthood and priestly celibacy all now began to enter the worship of the Western Church. These practices represented a mixing together of pagan elements of religion with biblical doctrines. When that kind of marriage takes place, the result is often not only a compromise of the faith, but an entirely different faith.

At the same time, Gregory's influence was also to be for the good of the church. He was profoundly interested in mission, in reaching out to unreached and unchartered territory with the message of Christ. Largely due to his influence at the end of the sixth century, missions were undertaken to England and to other parts of Europe, which, although spreading the influence and authority of Rome, also served the missionary interests of the gospel.

British Christianity

We have already noted that there is evidence of a Christian presence in Britain in the fourth century and the early fifth century. But it was during the sixth century in particular that the foundation was laid for the evangelisation of Scotland. There are two names of significance in this connection.

The first is the name of Augustine of Canterbury (d.604; not to be confused with Augustine, the Bishop of Hippo). He was commissioned by Gregory the Great as a missionary to England. The marriage of Aethelbert, the king of Kent, to a Christian princess, Bertha, gave Gregory the opportunity to establish a centre in the South of England. Augustine was prior of a monastery in Rome, and left Rome in 596. The following year he landed at Kent, and reached Canterbury, where Aethelbert and many of his people welcomed him and embraced the Christian faith. Augustine became bishop of Canterbury in 597, and this was the beginning of an episcopal seat in Canterbury, where today the primate of the Church of England has his throne. With the conversion of northern England, York became prominent as an ecclesiastical seat of power, which is why today the archbishops of Canterbury and York are the two senior figures in the Church of England. When Augustine arrived at Canterbury and was made primate of the See of Canterbury, there were already Christian bishops in England. By appointing Augustine over them, Gregory was consolidating the position of the papacy. So amid the political and ecclesiastical intrigue, the missionary cause of the gospel was, in fact, advancing.

The name with which many are familiar is that of Columba (521-597), the great sixth-century missionary to the Scots. Although Ninian had established his monastery on the Solway, it was Columba who was to evangelise most of Scotland. John Mackay, in his Chalmers Lectures on *The Church in the Highlands*, says:

> any lights that penetrated the spiritual and moral darkness which brooded over the Highlands and Islands of Alba, previous to the 12th May 563, were feeble and flickering. On that day, however, Columba took possession of one of our smaller isles, and made it a centre from which the light of the Gospel sent its cheering rays to every isle of the west.[51]

The language may be flowery, and may disguise the difficulties Columba faced, but it is true that from his centre at Iona, Columba was used by God to send the gospel message into remote parts of Scotland.

We know about the life of Columba chiefly from his biographer Adamnan, who was the ninth abbot of the monastery in Iona and who lived in the seventh century. Although Adamnan's account gives little detail about Columba's missionary activity, it is clear that he reached the north of Scotland, certainly coming as far as Skye. My first pastoral charge was in the parish of Snizort in Skye, where ruins of an old place of worship are still to be seen in an old graveyard on a small island in the River Snizort, called St Columba's Isle. Some of the local historians in Skye were of the view that St Columba's Isle and the ruins of the temple there represent what might have been another Iona. Historians talk of the Columban church in Scotland, which recognises that many of the practices of Iona were replicated throughout various centres of influence in Scotland, and the Columban Church became the vehicle through which the truth of the gospel was carried in our land in the sixth century.

Columba's main competitor for the soul of Scotland was Druidism. The Druids were the priests of an indigenous, practical religion among the Picts, and were hostile to Christianity. Columba is reputed to have been the means of the conversion of Brude, King of the Picts (although some historians challenge this). Brude lived near Inverness, and much of Columba's activity centred around Loch Ness. John Mackay says that 'the druidism of the Picts, so far as it held the place of a religion, fell quickly before the doctrines of Christianity',[52] although the paganism of Druidism is not completely exhausted from parts of Scotland. It is said that Columba established some forty Irish and some fifty Scottish churches, and his influence is reflected in the number of churches which bear the name of St Columba. By the end of the sixth century the light of the gospel had shone far into the northern reaches of Great Britain.

Other Significant Events

The Birth of Muhammad

The birth of Muhammad in Mecca, in 570, means that we can trace the rise of Islam to the end of the sixth century and the beginning of the seventh. We shall come back to this in the next chapter, but the life of Muhammad is an interesting one. By the end of the sixth century he had claimed to have had many ecstatic, spiritual experiences which convinced him to worship Allah.

The conversion of the Visigoths

We have already met the Visigoths – tribal Germans – in connection with their advance on Rome in 410 and Augustine's writing of his *City of God* as a result. By the mid-sixth century the Visigoths had advanced through Spain, and the conversion of Recared the Visigoth king of Spain to the Catholic faith in 589 marked a new opening and a new chapter in the history of Catholic Christianity in Europe. Part of the result of this was the repudiation of Arianism and the acceptance of the orthodox religion. These movements of history explain why Roman Catholicism is so strong in these parts of Europe.

The Seventh Century – Challenge

Important dates

627	Conversion of Northumbria
632	Death of Muhammad
649	Monothelitism condemned
664	Synod of Whitby bows to Rome over date of Easter

The rise of Islam

One of the features of the seventh century was the rise of the Islamic religion. Muhammad, as we have seen, was born in Mecca in 570, and lost his parents at an early age. He went off into the desert, and there he spent much time in prayer, and claimed to have ecstatic visions. He claimed that he was the true servant of Allah, the one true God, and that his mission was to empty Arabia of the polytheism and the idolatry which afflicted it.

There was opposition to his preaching, and in 622 he had to flee from Mecca to Medina. Muslims date their religion to Muhammad's journey to Medina. Nine years later he was welcomed to Mecca as a hero, and he had great influence there before he died in 632.

Muhammad began writing the Koran in around 610, and it was to become the sacred book of the Muslims. The word Koran means 'recitation', and it claims to be a record of words spoken by Gabriel to Muhammad, the prophet of Allah. Muslims would claim that they do not worship Muhammad; that they regard him as the greatest prophet (although they would regard Jesus as a prophet also). What the Koran did, however, was to lay down some clear and some stark rules by which Muslims are to live.

At the heart of Islam are the five pillars. First, there is the creed: 'There is no God but Allah and Muhammad is the prophet of Allah'. Second, there is prayer. Muslims must pray five times daily, always facing Mecca. Third, there is almsgiving; fourth, fasting; and fifth, pilgrimage. At least once in his life a Muslim should make a trip to Mecca. By these five pillars the Islam religion has remained bonded together, and has grown into a tight-knit and, sometimes, intolerant religion which is a major world religion today.

During the hundred years after Muhammad's death, Islam grew quickly, with its followers pursuing an aggressive policy of conversion by conquest. They took Damascus in 635, and by 640 the Muslims had entered Egypt. By 670 North Africa had been conquered. It is reckoned that were it not for the defeat of the Muslims by Charles Martel at Tours (France) in 732, they would have dominated Europe. This battle has been called 'one of the most decisive battles in history'.[53]

One historian has suggested that because Islam offered a way of life that was coherent and integrated, part of the effect of this rapid growth of Islam in the seventh century was that countries had either to embrace it or reject it in total.[54] Many Arabic and Eastern countries did embrace it unreservedly, while those nations that did not were then left to define and to defend their own position. The change was probably most marked in Europe, where the growth of coherent civilization developed, as much as a defence against Islam as an expression of integrated Christianity.

The Monothelite controversy

The theological controversies of the previous centuries spilled over into the seventh. The famous *filioque* (= 'and from the Son') clause, adopted by the Council of Toledo in 589, affirmed that the Holy Spirit proceeded from the Father *and from the Son*. It was only one word, but it continued to polarise east and west, with the Eastern Church refusing to accept the procession of the Spirit from any but the Father alone.

Controversies surrounding the Person of Christ continued into the seventh century. One of the questions which remained unresolved after Chalcedon was the question of whether Christ had one will or two. This is a question about the relation between the two natures of Christ, both of which Chalcedon emphasised as being distinct, with each retaining its properties after the incarnation. To say that Christ had only one will seemed to confuse the natures; those who said Christ had two wills seemed to separate the natures, if not make Christ into two Persons.

A group known as the monothelites (one will) arose within the church. Some of these said that the human will of Christ was merged in the divine, and that it was his divine will that acted. Others said that Christ's will was singular, but a fusion of divine and human.

The doctrine that Christ had one will was a minority position, and it was condemned at the Council of Constantinople in 680-1. The view that Christ had two wills has been the majority view held in the church since. Charles Hodge says:

> since intelligence, sensibility and will are the properties of the human soul, without which it ceases to be a soul, it follows that the human soul of Christ retained its intelligence, sensibility and will. But intelligence and will are no less the essential properties of the divine nature and thus were retained after its union with the human nature in Christ. Therefore, in teaching that Christ was truly man and truly God, the Scriptures teach that He had a finite intelligence and an infinite intelligence. Moreover, in Him *there were and are two wills or operations.* His human intellect increased; his divine intelligence was and is infinite. His human will had only human power; his divine will was and is almighty.[55]

We are told in the Bible that Jesus knew what was in man (John 2:25), that is, he had a knowledge that penetrated the hearts of men, a divine omniscience. Yet at the same time there were some things he did not know. Similarly, Jesus could command nature and say to the winds and waves 'peace, be still', a prerogative and a power which belong only to God. Yet he could also say to his Father in the garden of Gethsemane, 'not my will, but your will be done.'

Monothelitism grew out of the idea that if you begin with the unity of Christ's Person you must say that he had only one will. But the theological difficulty lies in the fact that Christ had 'come to be what he was not, without ceasing to be what he was'. He did not empty himself of his divine attributes when he became man. He retained the power to will at a divine level. But servanthood represents a modification, a recasting of Sonship. As the servant, commissioned to save those whom the Father gave him, Christ voluntarily chose to please the Father and voluntarily chose what no human being could ever wish for.[56] In discussing this point of doctrine, Wayne Grudem says that 'failing to understand something does not mean that it is impossible, only that our understanding is limited'.[57] All of which requires of us tremendous care when presenting points of doctrine; not least, when speaking about the Person of our Lord.

In the Western Church, another controversy had arisen which was called Adoptionism. This was the view that Christ had been 'adopted' by God as to his humanity, and that Christ's humanity had been assumed into his divinity. This was one way in which an attempt was made to safeguard the unity of Christ's Person; but it was really an early heresy in a new form. A Council at Toledo in Spain in 675 affirmed, however, that Christ was Son of God by nature, and not by adoption.

Continuing missionary activity in Europe and Britain
At the end of the sixth century, the See of Canterbury had been established, and Columba had begun his missionary work throughout Scotland. Missionary work in Northumbria led to the establishment of York as a centre of episcopalianism by the beginning of the seventh century. By the 650s, the English Church, with a distinctive episcopalian structure, had been established. Some of the monks from Iona had established Lindisfarne, in Northumbria, also named the Holy Island, around 635. Lindisfarne was called a 'new Iona', and was established by Aidan (d. 651). Christianity spread throughout north England, and indeed into parts of Europe from Lindisfarne. Northumbria became an important Christian centre in Europe. It was in Northumbria that the great church historian, Bede (later known as the Venerable Bede) was born in 672.

One of the great figures of the seventh century was Columbanus (c.543-615), who in the early years of the seventh century had done much to pursue the evangelisation of France and parts of Britain.[58] He worked out from Bangor in Ireland, and had laboured in Italy, Switzerland and France. He had, among other things, challenged the Pope on the question of the true date of Easter, showing that there was an independent mindset and spirit here which was running in an opposite direction to that of Rome, and which could challenge the claims and doctrines of European Christianity. The result was confusion between the indigenous Celtic Christians and the Latin Roman Church.

On some issues it was difficult for the Celtic Christian movement and the episcopalian movement to find common ground. There were difficulties regarding the attitude of the two different wings of British Christianity to the pope, for example, with some regarding Rome as an ecclesiastical seat of authority, and others regarding it as a purely judicial centre of authority.

King Oswy of Northumbria called an important Synod in Whitby in North East England in 664. One of the main issues that made this Synod necessary was the dispute over the proper dating of religious festivals. Renwick summarises: 'representatives of the Roman and Celtic communions discussed their differences; King Oswy of Northumbria was won over to the side of the Church of Rome. From then onwards the influence of the Celtic Church gradually waned throughout Britain but many traces of its great work remained for centuries.'[59]

There was a retreat by the Celtic monks away from Lindisfarne to Iona and the Romanising of Britain was much advanced. Some have argued that the significance of Whitby was negligible, and was little more than a private quarrel. Nevertheless, it was significant in terms of bringing the English church into line with Roman practice.

The seventh century was a time of great change: it was a time when the loose federalism of the tribal structures of Britain was giving way to something more concrete and robust. The development of something akin to a parish system is evident in the way in which, from this time, the bishops were understood to have a rectoral and pastoral influence over the people as a whole. The church thus came to be regarded as a means of social control and of social influence. When Theodore of Tarsus became archbishop of Canterbury in 668, he established the church as a 'national body', reorganizing the church as a governor of social and secular life. The church thus came to be seen as a central and unifying power.

Archbishop Theodore was also interested in encouraging culture, learning and scholarship. When he founded a school at Canterbury, the arts and humanities flourished. Bede himself was a product of this system, and biblical studies were greatly encouraged. The production of the Lindisfarne Gospels and, later, the Book of Kells, important sources for our knowledge of the Christianity of the medieval period, can be traced to the influence of Theodore's school.

One of the features of this period, as we saw with Columbanus, is the missionary movement out of Britain and into parts of Europe, including parts of Italy and Germany. So by the seventh century we are seeing not only the consolidation of British Christianity as a result of influences *from* Europe; we are also seeing the evangelisation of parts of Europe by Irish-Celtic missionaries. One of these was Wynfrith of Crediton (680-754), also known as Boniface, to whom we shall return in the next chapter. Another prominent missionary to Europe was Willibrord of York, who lived to see many of the Frankish tribes embrace Christianity. He became archbishop of Utrecht in 695.

Important Influences
Vivian Green, in *A New History of Christianity*, says that

> the mainspring of Christianity between the sixth and the eighth centuries continued to be found in the monasteries, more especially in the monasteries of Celtic Ireland where Christian societies preserved ancient learning, and became centres of a rigorous asceticism and of enthusiasm for the propagation of the Christian Gospel.[60]

These monasteries were self-sufficient, and were centres of learning through which the Word of God continued to be preserved even through the darkest of ages. It is estimated that by 600, there were some 220 monasteries in France alone, with a further 320 added during the seventh century.[61]

The period up until around 800 is generally known as the Dark Ages, because of the relatively low state of learning, and the prevalence of barbarism.[62] But even in the seventh century, we can see Christian themes reflected in some aspects of popular culture. In Eastern Europe, scholarship and learning remained strong, although a council held in the palace of Trullum in Constantinople in 692 banned any new interpretations of the Bible. It seems that they had had enough of controversy! But generally in the British Isles the monasteries, and later Theodore's school of learning, combined to produce some biblical scholars of note even in these times.

- One of the outstanding theologians of the period was Isidore of Seville (c.560-636), who was a leader of the Spanish church from 600 to 636. He wrote brief commentaries on several biblical books, and also left to the medieval church his *Books of Sentences*, which were brief doctrinal statements, and his *Etymologies*, which was an encyclopedic compilation of the teachings of earlier Christian leaders and which became a standard reference work for the later church.

- Another important figure was Maximus the Confessor (c.580-662), whose work in the seventh century laid the foundation for later allegorising tendencies in the Eastern Church. Although his approach to Scripture owed more to his work in philosophy than to his theology, he nonetheless believed that it was necessary to master the whole of the Bible, believing that the deepest and most important questions in the universe could be answered there. In his extreme old age he was imprisoned for his faith, and had his right hand cut off and his tongue cut out.

- An influential scholar in Britain was Aldhelm of Malmesbury (c.640-709), who became bishop in the new diocese of Sherborne. He was important for his work on the Psalter, which reflects both Celtic and Roman influences.

Gerald Bray suggests that 'it was in the area of commentary-writing that this period displayed the least originality'.[63] In other words, the scholars of the period were not really writing new or ground-breaking material. But they were preserving the truth, and preserving interpretations of the truth which had been prominent in the earlier period. It is to such men that we owe, under God, the maintenance of a Bible-centred religion and lifestyle which ensured the continuance of the church even amid the darkness of the period.

The Eighth Century – Christendom

Important dates

716	Boniface's first missionary journey
726	Beginnings of iconoclastic controversy
731	Bede's *Ecclesiastical History*
771	Charlemagne becomes sole ruler of France
793	Lindisfarne sacked

The term, 'the Dark Ages,' is a suitable designation for the period on which we are reflecting, not least because the light of gospel truth was severely dimmed, and the work of the church was limited to the preservation of the gospel in a world characterised by invasion, hostility, barbarism, immorality and ignorance. One historian calls the leaders of the church in this period 'Christians of the twilight',[64] because of the situation in which the church worked and witnessed.

The church not only made important theological and religious contributions during this period, but also expended much energy for the social good of the people. The church undertook to help those who lived in social deprivation, and who were in need of charity. That she continued to do so under the growing dominion and threat of Islam, highlights the faithfulness of God. Some of the important African centres of Christianity fell to Islam early in the eighth century, with some Spanish cities succumbing to Muslim conquest soon after. It is reckoned that during this period, 90% of Spain fell to Islam.

Bede's History
In the previous chapter, we noted the birth of Bede in Northumbria. He entered a monastery and received his theological training within the monastic system. During his lifetime he scarcely moved away from the place of his birth, and most of his knowledge was gained from the monastery library. He was a biographer of Cuthbert of

Lindisfarne. It was late in his life, in 731, that he wrote his famous *Ecclesiastical History*, and it represents one of the highest points of intellectual culture in the Western Church in the eighth century. This book was written to trace the development of the church in England, and Bede wrote it in the style of the Old Testament narratives which traced the fortunes of Israel as they related to the kings. From the idealising spirit of his writings it is difficult to argue that this is pure research, nevertheless it is an important resource for seeing how Christianity in the north of England became so diverse, and so different to the Mediterranean countries from which it had originally sprung.

The missionary labours of Boniface

Another famous British monk, Boniface (680-754), was responsible for carrying the gospel into parts of Europe, most notably into the Germanic areas. Boniface visited Rome in 718-19 and it was from the pope that he received a commission to labour in Germany. He was made an archbishop in 732 and became subservient to the pope. Not only was his work in Europe successful, but through his influence many of the Irish monks were brought into subservience to Rome. He founded a monastery which was to be a centre of 'learning and priestly education for all western-central Germany'.[65] Although he strengthened the authority of the pope, he was influential in spreading the doctrines of the truth and in bringing discipline and order into the church. Many travelled from England to help him in the work, and to devote themselves to a monastic lifestyle and Christian service. In this way, the English church by the eighth century was returning missionaries to Europe, having originally received the gospel from Europe.

Boniface was responsible for calling various synods from 742 onwards. He was concerned for the worldliness of the priests, the marriage of priests, and the lack of clerical discipline. At such a synod in 747, the authority of the pope was recognised. Much of his influence was to be found in the improvement of the organization, character and discipline of the church.

Boniface always maintained a missionary interest and a missionary spirit. It was with such a spirit that he travelled to Frisia in 754, where he was martyred, 'thus crowning his active and widely influential life with a death of witness to his faith. His work had been one for order, discipline and consolidation, as well as Christian advancement, and these were the chief needs of the age.'[66]

Other Christian leaders of the eighth century

- John of Damascus (c.650-754), sometimes known as John Damascene, ministered in Damascus and Palestine. He was born to Christian parents, and received ordination following a political career. He wrote a work of theology entitled *Source of Knowledge*, which became a standard theological work for the Eastern Church.

- Alcuin (c.735-804) ministered in York and Tours (France). He was born into a very well-to-do family, and was educated at the Cathedral School of York. During his lifetime he wrote a Life of St Willibrord and also produced a revision of Jerome's Vulgate translation.

Important developments in France

During the eighth century an important alliance developed between the Papacy and the rulers of France. It was in the interests of Rome to secure such an alliance, because of the threat to Rome from different places. The various kings of France also wanted to have the moral support of Rome and the Papacy over issues which were affecting them.

In 768, Charlemagne (742-814) succeeded his father as emperor. He was a skilled and clever man, who believed that his authority was derived from God, and that his political power ought to go hand in hand with ecclesiastical power. He looked on the clergy as a means by which he could train and reform society for the service of God. He was also responsible for regularising the worship and liturgy of the Western Church.

On Christmas Day, 800, the pope crowned Charlemagne as emperor of the Holy Roman Empire of the West. This was the culmination of the developments of the eighth century, during which the Papacy had advanced its claim of temporal sovereignty. Charlemagne had saved the pope from Lombard invasion, and had also delivered him in 799 from the anger of Rome, whose population had accused him of many faults. The crowning of Charlemagne was a potent symbol of the idea of one state and one church, with the emperor and the Pope working together. This is what gives us the concept of 'Christendom', the concept of 'a world that is a church', of political and religious power governing the lives and the worship of people.

H. Daniel-Rops summarises:

> In 800, after thirty-two years of his reign, Charlemagne appeared to embody a glory which no man had equalled for centuries. He had forced Islam back beyond the Alps and had imposed his rule upon the whole of the civilised West. He had been the great converter as well as the great conqueror...Thanks to him Western Christianity was extended and strengthened... And he possessed much more than temporal glory. He possessed exceptional moral prestige: no sovereign since Constantine had assembled so many territories beneath his sceptre; like Constantine he appeared to mankind as the witness, as the herald, of Christ.[67]

The alliance worked well during Charlemagne's time, but became open to abuse in later times. Charlemagne sought to use his power to regulate the lives of the priests and to set up schools throughout the land. This led to what has been termed the *Charlemagne Renaissance*, a period during which learning flourished, and during which the foundation was laid for the great humanistic scholarship of the Middle Ages.

The iconoclast controversy

One of the important controversies of the eighth century centred on the use of pictures and images in Christian worship. This affected the church both in the West and in the East, but the centre of the controversy was particularly in Byzantium, in the Eastern Church. The development of art meant that increasingly Christian symbols were appearing in churches, and the idea behind their use was that 'seeing leads to faith'. These pictures appeared not only in places of worship, but also in private homes, in shops, on clothes and in jewellery. Some superstitiously maintained that God himself had created them miraculously. They became objects not only of admiration, but of veneration in themselves, of worship and of adoration. Their use in the Eastern Church signalled at one level the end of barbarism and an intellectual revival; on the other hand, the use of icons and images was to precipitate a long ecclesiastical crisis.

The Eastern Emperor Leo III (Byzantine Emperor from 717 to 740) had successfully prevented the Muslims from capturing Constantinople in 718. He enacted that images were idolatrous and ought to be destroyed. This edict may have been in part designed to appease the Muslims, who would allow no physical representation of God, but was ostensibly passed on theological grounds – to depict Christ as a man, it was argued, could not show that he was also God. A human representation of Jesus, therefore, was in effect a separation of his two natures. This was an interesting counter-argument to the view of John Damascene that the incarnation actually shows that God made it possible to paint the portrait of a man. Many in the East embraced this view, considering that a church was not truly a holy place unless it was adorned with images and icons as aids to worship and faith.

Leo began his campaign against images in 726. He seems to have had a genuine spiritual concern over the veneration of images but his position led to disturbances throughout the empire: *iconoclasm* is the practice of image-breaking, hence the 'iconoclast controversy'. The word 'iconoclast' is now used metaphorically to describe anyone who wants to 'destroy' an accepted idea or belief. Pope Gregory II condemned these measures. The debate over images therefore soon became a debate over the respective roles of church and state. When the religious leaders and people revolted against Leo's ban on images, he used arms to enforce it. Constantine V, Leo's son, continued the harsh measures of his father. At a council in 754, Constantine persecuted those who revered images.

The Second General Council of Nicaea was convened in 787, largely through the influence of Irene, the wife of Leo IV, and proclaimed that while it was unlawful to worship images, it was necessary to venerate them, to give them respect and attention. But this did not heal the conflict between church and state; nor did it prevent iconoclasm in the following century. Indeed, Charlemagne called an anti-images meeting at Frankfurt in 794. The Council represented the interest of the emperor in the flowering of art and culture, but at the same time showed the departure from the Bible which characterised the medieval church of this period.

Viking invasions

In the 790s a series of Viking invasions were the scourge of the monasteries. The Scandinavian raiders attacked the monasteries not because they were anti-Christian, but because they believed that the monasteries contained treasure and money. There is not much evidence to suggest that the monasteries were overly rich, but a high standard of life was enjoyed within their walls, coupled with theological study and religious devotion. But one historian has suggested that a 'late seventh- or an eighth- century monastery often had many of the aspects of a special kind of nobleman's club'.[68] The Vikings attacked Lindisfarne in 793 and Iona in 795. Many churches in northern England were also threatened, and Viking ships soon sailed to France and threatened Paris.

Some saw the hand of God in the Viking invasions, and saw them as an expression of God's anger at sin. There were some brave attempts to encourage Christians to remain faithful to Christ, and many did.

The Ninth Century – Darkness

Important dates

800   Charlemagne crowned Holy Roman Emperor
814   Reform of the monasteries
863-7   The Photian schism

The eighth century had witnessed the growing alliance between France and the Papacy, culminating in the crowning of Charlemagne on Christmas Day 800 by Pope Leo at St Peter's in Rome. This marked the beginning of the Holy Roman Empire, and in the course of the ninth century, Charlemagne extended his kingdom. The pope benefited from Charlemagne's military strength, which allowed the Papacy to gain previously unconquered lands. The Roman Empire in the West had been destroyed, yet the idea of empire remained a popular and powerful ideal, as a Christian, centralised basis of power and government. Many saw in Charlemagne a rebirth of Constantine, and were willing to give him their support.

Charlemagne's motto was: 'It is my duty, with the help of the divine Mercy, to defend the Holy Church of God with my arms, everywhere.' One historian has said that

> all his life Charlemagne was magnificently faithful to the mission which he expressed in these words. Mounted on his horse, sword in hand, the tireless leader pursued this ideal of the Christian warrior as long as he lived. In the 45 years of his reign he made no less than 55 expeditions; he was still fighting six months before his death.[69]

Despite the problems caused by this close liaison between Church and State, Christian Europe was protected and extended under Charlemagne. At the same time, he pursued a policy of conversion by terror, forcing people to accept Christianity under threat of violence. Some stalwart theologians and leaders sought to counsel Charlemagne to 'preach before baptising', rather than coerce people into embracing Christianity. However, even in the terror of these campaigns, a gospel work was done: the seed of Christianity was planted in lands 'where Charles' [Charlemagne's] sword had parted the furrow'.[70]

Charlemagne died in 814, and he became a legend in the ninth century. He had brought order into the civilisations of Europe, and had been responsible for sponsoring a cultural and intellectual renaissance. The bishops said that 'he shone like gold'. The reality was shrouded under the myth, however, and when his leadership was no longer there, violence once again broke out in the name of Christianity.

Bible Scholarship during the ninth century

Gerald Bray has written that in the ninth century, 'biblical studies hardly progressed at all, except in quantity'.[71] The work on Bible interpretation was heavily dependent on the earlier patristic writers, and little was done by way of original formulation. The following names were prominent during this period:

- Claudius of Turin (died c. 827) became Bishop of Turin in 816. He opposed the veneration of the saints and the idea of papal supremacy. He was accused of being an Adoptionist, but the accusation could not be proven. He wrote commentaries on many Old and New Testament books, and was widely acclaimed as a theologian and biblical scholar of note.

- Haymo of Auxerre (died c.855) wrote commentaries on the Song of Songs, the minor prophets, the epistles of Paul and Revelation. His writings were to be widely used in the Middle Ages.

- Rabanus Maurus (c.780-856) also produced several commentaries. He was very dependent on Origen, the allegorist, and was held to be the father of German scholarship. He also wrote a manual for priests.

- Remigius of Auxerre (c.841-908) wrote short, clear commentaries. In his exposition of the Book of Psalms he sought to apply the psalms to the society of his day. These references to the contemporary world show that he had a strong pastoral concern.

- Paschasius Radbertus (c.785-865) was a monk in Corbie, near Amiens (France), who was skilled in both Greek and Latin theology. He was one of the first Western writers to engage in discussion of the Eucharist, or Lord's Supper, publishing a treatise on this subject in 831. To the extent that this had not been done before, he was an original thinker, which marked him apart from many of his contemporaries. His works provoked a great deal of controversy, particularly because of his emphasis on the change of the substance of the bread and wine in the act of participation. He wished to retain the Latin emphasis of Augustine that only by faith can a person partake of the Lord's Supper in a fitting manner; but to this he added the Greek notion of eating the food of immortality. He argued that by a divine miracle, the elements are transformed into the very body and blood of Christ. This laid the foundation for the official doctrine of transubstantiation, which was adopted as dogma in 1215.

This controversy produced some able defences of the orthodox doctrine of the Sacrament. One was by Ratramnus of Corbie (d. 825), a fellow-monk of Radbertus, who argued that as far as the substance of the elements was concerned, 'they are after the consecration what they were before.'[72] Ratramnus argued that the Sacrament is received invisibly and by faith. He said that what was present in the Sacrament was not the body which the virgin conceived and bore, but the power of the divine Word, a spiritual body, suited to the occasion of the Sacrament itself. Although Ratramnus was raised as a defender of the orthodox, biblical doctrine, the Roman church opted for the doctrine of the sacraments argued by Radbertus.

- John Scotus Erigena (c. 810-77). John Scotus was an Irishman of Scottish descent, who flourished in the intellectual renaissance after Charlemagne. He had a detailed knowledge of Greek theology,

and detected various discrepancies between the Greek fathers
and the Latin theologians of his own day. He translated several
patristic works into Latin. John Scotus questioned some of the
acknowledged experts and also taught that the sayings of the fathers
were subject to the teachings of Scripture. One of his emphases
was on the spiritual nature of the Sacrament. It was not enough to
receive the Lord's Supper; it was necessary to exercise faith in
the receiving of it. We receive the Sacrament 'mentally, not
dentally'. John Scotus was rightly hailed as one of the great
theologians of the Middle Ages, who set forth a philosophical system
for understanding the universe. Some of his work was condemned
by later church councils, but he was a powerful thinker in his day.

A controversy over the doctrine of predestination arose around
the writings of Gottschalk of Orbais (c.803-68). A student of
Augustine, Gottschalk accepted Augustine's doctrine of double
predestination, teaching that both the saved and the lost are
predestinated to their respective ends. Gregory the Great had
influenced earlier views on the subject by teaching a predestination
only in respect of the elect, based on God's foreknowledge. But
Gottschalk argued that there is a double predestination, and that God's
power is limited to the objects of redemption. God's decrees, he argued,
are not dependent on the will or the actions of man.

Gottschalk met with much opposition. He was accused of making
God the author of sin. A council at Mainz in 848 condemned his
teaching (for which he was later deposed as a priest), and led to a
debate between some of the leading theologians of the ninth century.
A church council at Valence in 855 supported Gottschalk's view. One
historian points out the irony that although the West was being torn
apart by invasions and civil strife, the church was able to debate and
discuss such points. Perhaps that was a sign that there was life and
light in her yet.

Continued missionary movement

In the ninth century, the missionary work of the church continued.
We read of the unevangelised areas of Europe being reached with
the gospel. For example, Cyril (826-869) and his brother Methodius

(c.815-885) from Thessalonica were working in the East. They were called the 'Apostles of the Slavs', because they worked in Moravia from about 864 onwards. Cyril prepared for this work by inventing a written form of the Slavic language, which became the foundation of the Russian alphabet and was used to translate the gospel into the Slavic tongue. Moravia became a centre of Christian influence from the end of the ninth century onwards.

There is also record of a missionary Ansgar (801-865), nicknamed the Apostle of the North, because he entered Denmark in 826 with the gospel. He was only there a short time before he was driven out. In 829-830 he laboured in Sweden, and the pope appointed him archbishop of Hamburg in 831 as a base for the evangelisation of Scandinavia. Though he was removed from there in 845, when Hamburg was destroyed by the Danes, he simply became bishop of Bremen, from where he continued his activities.

Photius

Meanwhile, relations between Rome and the East of the Empire had become strained because of a schism which centred around Photius (c. 810-90). In 858 the Emperor Michael III had appointed Photius, a distinguished civil servant, as patriarch of Constantinople, in place of Ignatius. Ignatius appealed against this to the pope, who excommunicated Photius. Photius in turn called a synod to protest against Rome's unwarranted interference in this affair, and declared in 867 that the pope had deposed himself and excommunicated himself through his actions. The bitter strife went on for several years; a council at Constantinople in 869 deposed Photius; the emperor restored him to office in 877; and the emperor Leo VI deposed him again in 886.

This was, however, more than a political struggle internal to the Eastern Empire. It was a dispute over the legitimate authority of the church. The Roman Church asserted its claim that it had rightful jurisdiction over the Eastern Church, but the result was that the rift between the two became even wider. When the Pope disallowed the Slavonic liturgy in 885, it was the catalyst which severely strained relationships between the churches on both sides of the empire.

Photius also involved the Eastern Church in a further theological controversy over the 'filioque' clause. The Eastern Church claimed that the West had added the words 'and from the Son' to the Nicene creed in respect of the procession of the Holy Spirit. This, along with a controversy over the use of unleavened bread in the Sacrament, led to the deepening of the divide.

Photius' writings became immensely popular; he was one of the first thinkers and theologians who publicly challenged Rome's claim to supremacy in the church. One of his pamphlets was entitled 'Against those who say that Rome is the premier See'.

Nicolas I

One of the leading churchmen of the time, however, was Pope Nicolas I, Pope from 858 to 867. He has been described as the 'first great Medieval Pope'. He had been secretary to Pope Benedict III and succeeded him in 858. Nicolas is described as 'handsome of face, strict in morals and generous in habits', a man who 'combined a marvellous wisdom with qualities of energy and courage'.[73]

When one of the kings of Italy, Lothaire II, divorced his wife with the approval of his local bishops, Nicolas intervened to uphold Christian principles in this tense political situation. He had the courage to stand up to the king, affirming that marriage was indissoluble, and ordered him to take back his wife. The whole business was followed by a series of events which led to Nicolas himself being in danger for his life at one point, but his moral courage and steadfastness had a controlling effect throughout the empire. Lothaire did take his wife back, and Nicolas prevented a war within the family. A council held in Rome in 865, in the midst of Norse invasions of Europe and uncertainty and instability on every side, showed that Nicolas did have the moral authority to rule in Europe. He did oppose the appointment of Photius as patriarch because he believed that the imperial power had gone too far in appointing him.

So although this was an age of laxity and spiritual darkness, men like Nicolas were used as beacons of light and of truth. He often repeated the principle that guided him in his life and in his position: 'the things of the spirit triumph over the things of the world inasmuch as the spirit is superior to the flesh.' His nine-year pontificate was one of superior moral leadership, and his character, unlike many popes before or since, seems to have been exemplary. He wished to assert that the Church's leadership was centred on Rome.

Christianity in Britain

In Britain in the ninth century, the Columban-Celtic church had more or less been devastated by the Viking invasions. The Norsemen not only devastated the islands and robbed them of their population; they also destroyed many of the centres of Christianity. There were some heroic stories of martyrdom for the faith during the first years of the ninth century. A significant event took place in 843 with the crowning of Kenneth MacAlpine as king of a united kingdom of Picts and Scots, establishing his court at Scone in Perthshire. He built an important church at Dunkeld with the idea of having the Columban Church as the church of his kingdom, and having the Dunkeld church as the principal centre of Christian worship. He also wished to be independent of the Church of Rome. MacAlpine was responsible for moving some of the relics of Columba to Dunkeld.

Little evidence remains for the development of the Scottish church during this period. Monasticism had its defects, as it had its strengths. The earliest church in Scotland had much that was not biblical, yet was used to communicate the message of the truths of the gospel. There was, in the medieval world, a sense of God. The church was 'at the very centre of human existence'.[74] Although many areas of church life had been corrupted, and although the message of the gospel had often been compromised, the light of the gospel penetrated even the Dark Ages.

The Tenth Century – Instability

```
Important dates

910      Founding of the Abbey at Cluny
959      Dunstan becomes Archbishop of Canterbury
963      Ethelwold becomes Bishop of Winchester
995      The conversion of Norway
```

We are now almost halfway through our studies in the history of the church over two thousand years. The tenth century takes us to the last century of the first millennium, in which the church was called to minister in an age of darkness, of immorality, of barbarian invasion, when civilisation was in the twilight.

Gerald Bray tells us that the tenth century was 'a complete blank' as far as biblical scholarship was concerned, 'because theologians turned their attention to other matters, notably the development of the liturgy'.[75] Serious biblical scholarship really begins at the commencement of the second millennium, from the eleventh century onwards.

An unstable papacy

One of the features of the early tenth century was the instability of the papacy. We saw in the last couple of chapters that the invasions of various tribes threatened the peace of Italy, which drew the pope more and more into political controversy. The popes of the time showed themselves generally unfit for the responsibility of guiding the church through the political upheavals and unrest of the period. In the first half of the tenth century, there were no less than seventeen successive popes. This instability resulted from the papacy being embroiled in dynastic politics. The clan Theophylact exercised particularly powerful influence. Theophylact was a consul and senator at the same time as being financial director of the holy see. He was assisted by his ambitious wife Theodora. After their deaths, power concentrated in the hands of their even more ambitious and ruthless daughter, Marozia.

The tenth century saw the power of Germany growing, and the king, Otto, followed in Charlemagne's footsteps by being crowned Emperor by the Pope in 962. So there was instability throughout the empire, and instability also in the church.

Age of reform

One of the things, however, that does mark out the tenth century is that it was an era of reform. We have seen how the work of the gospel and the publication of the Scriptures focused largely upon the monasteries, where men worked and studied. Charlemagne had supported the monasteries because of their educational value. Their attraction is not difficult to see in a world full of misery, and torn apart by civil disorder.

A famous monastery was established in 910 at Cluny, in France. The monastery was to be self-sufficient, under the jurisdiction of the pope but free from any ecclesiastical or civil interference. The Benedictine Rule was to be followed, and was to be adhered to with a great strictness.

The first two abbots of the Monastery at Cluny, Berno (910-27) and Odo (927-42), were men of ability and of strong character, who governed the monastery well. So much was their influence felt there, that Cluny became a model for other monasteries throughout Europe. And although it began as an independent institution, whose main function was monastic reform by example – the vision that other monasteries would follow Cluny and be organised along the same lines – gradually, several monasteries came to be dependent on Cluny. The abbot there became the head of a 'congregation' of monasteries. This was a new development and led to various groupings of monastic communities.

The strength of this is to be seen in the influence the monasteries had on the French nobles. They were constantly warring and fighting, but one later abbot prescribed a period of cessation from fighting in memory of Christ's passion. This was called the 'Truce of God', and the success of it, though short-lived, shows the extent to which the reform of monastic life influenced the political life of the period.

With the reform of the monasteries, there went a desire for reform in the clergy generally. The monks and clerics within the Cluny movement stood opposed to various unethical practices which were current among the clergy. Around this time we read of simony (named after Simon the sorcerer of Acts 8), the practice of clerical services being rendered simply for financial or other gain, and of Nicolaitanism (from Revelation 2), which came to be the term to describe any breach of clerical celibacy (although it is doubtful whether this was the original meaning of the term 'Nicolaitans' in the New Testament). The Cluny party were against these. 'These reformers desired a worthy clergy, appointed for spiritual reasons, as the age understood worthiness.'[76]

It was not just at Cluny that such reform was taking place. In Lorraine, France, in the first half of the tenth century, Gerhard, the abbot of Brogne, began the reform of monasteries in his area. In the second half of the century we find Romuald of Ravenna organizing ascetic centres called 'deserts', which were probably much stricter than the monasteries, but which also became centres of evangelisation.

These movements were small, but were remarkable in a world characterised by immorality and ignorance. There was a genuine attempt to make the monastic system one which would serve the church well and which would make it more spiritual. These laid the foundation for the thorough-going reforms of Pope Leo IX in the next century.

It was a time of reform not only on the European mainland, but also within the British church, largely as a result of contact with the European monasteries. One of the reformers of the period was Dunstan, archbishop of Canterbury from 959 to 988. Another was Ethelwold, who was bishop of Winchester. He was influenced by the reforms at Cluny. Ethelwold drew up a new version of monastic rules, the *Regularis Concordia*. Ethelwold was also committed to the reform of the liturgy and we read of him having organs constructed at Abingdon and Winchester. The monasteries became more committed to spiritual exercises and more devoted to worthwhile intellectual pursuits. So, as Vivian Green writes, 'It is impossible to know how deeply this religious revival penetrated into parochial England, but the monks who became bishops tried to raise the standards of the parish priests, emphasising the celibacy of the clergy and the need to repress drunkenness and concubinage.'[77]

Some of the popes of the period were brave men, who fought against invaders and who lived to protect their people. Others, such as Pope John XIII (965-72), gave support to those in the far western reaches of Europe who wished to see the church reformed. At the very end of the tenth century we come across Pope Silvester II, who was pope for only three years (999-1002), at the turn of the millennium, and who was also the first French pope. Having been influenced by the reforms of the Cluny Order, he retained self-discipline and asceticism even as pope, setting an example and advocating reform. So again, God protected and preserved his church, even in a dark and uncivilised world. At the same time, we find the church corrupted in many ways with an idolatrous liturgy, and with unbiblical elements entering her life and service. One of these, which dates from the tenth century, is the introduction of *cardinals* within the church. These were the clergy who attended as servants to the pope, and who worked for the good of the church. The word *cardo* meant a *hinge*; the cardinals were understood to be the hinges of the church.

The Eastern Church

The iconoclastic controversy was one of the features of the eighth-century Eastern Church. It was symptomatic of an ongoing controversy in the East (see Photius in the ninth century) over the relationship between church and state, and the legitimate limits of the jurisdiction of both. But the Eastern church also had some able scholars at this time. One, Simeon Metaphrastes, edited a collection of the lives of the saints at this period. He was a mystic, who lived into the eleventh century. Tradition has it that as he contemplated God in his monastery, he had such a vision of God that he was surrounded by the light that appeared at the Mount of Transfiguration.

Another controversy which came to a head in the Eastern church at this time was over the Paulicians, whose origins are obscure. Their movement seems to have absorbed elements from ancient heresies, such as Marcionism and Gnosticism; they were dualists, who held to a separation between the world, which is evil, and all that comes from God, which is good. By the tenth century they had spread rapidly and had amassed military power, so that by 969 the Emperor was settling them in various places and looked to them for a defence against invading Bulgarians.

The Eastern Empire was consolidating itself at this point, increasing in military might and strength, and under a succession of powerful leaders, generally becoming stronger.

Christian advance

The tenth century was also a time of Christian extension and expansion. We have already noted the work of Ansgar in Scandinavia. It did not have many results, but it did lead to a further spread of Christianity. In the tenth century, the work was followed by Unni, the archbishop of Hamburg (918-36) and by Archbishop Adaldag (937-88). The king of Denmark embraced Christianity during the course of the century, and soon churches were established and bishops settled in Denmark. Norway was also evangelised in the middle of the tenth century, and at the end of the century, English preachers had come in and had permanently settled the Christian church there.

This was to have repercussions for all the lands under Scandinavian control, including Orkney, Shetland and the Hebrides. Murdo Macaulay alludes to this in his *Aspects of the Religious History of Lewis*, where he says that 'in 875 Christianity was practically extinguished in the northern isles...but in 997 it was reintroduced by... Olaf. Olaf was the first king of Norway who embraced Christianity. He compelled his people to be baptized, and to accept the Christian faith.'[78] At this time the Hebrides were known as the bishopric of Sodor. The Norse influence on the islands is well-known, and survives in many of the place-names there. It was about this time that Christianity re-established itself in these Scottish islands.

In the tenth century, St Andrews became the prominent Christian site of Scotland. Dunkeld, which had been the centre of MacAlpine's reign, had been destroyed by the Vikings in 903, and St Andrews became the principal church.

These expansionist movements were largely the work of the Western Church. The Eastern Church also was growing in this period, and one of the great achievements of the tenth century was the bringing of Christianity to Russia. Russian merchants had probably seen the splendours of the buildings occupied by the Eastern Church, and came back with stories of the magnificent buildings. In turn, Christian missionaries were able to gain access to Russia and to plant a work

ne of the main events in the tenth century was the conversion
ptism of Vladimir, king of Russia in 988. This was celebrated in
Russia in 1988 under the motto 'One Thousand Years of Christianity
in Russia', with even the atheistic communist party acknowledging it.
The Russian Orthodox Church was established, with its centre in
Kiev. Eventually Moscow was to become the acknowledged centre
of Russian Christianity.

Speculation regarding the end of world in 1,000

There is evidence to suggest that some extreme thinkers of the period
fully expected the world to end in the year 1,000. They based this
speculation on texts such as 'one day is with the Lord as a thousand
years, and a thousand years as one day', and on the word of Revelation
that God would bind Satan for one thousand years. They believed
that God's terrible day of judgement had arrived. This was not a
universal view within the church, but it was present, and it was echoed
in several speculative views as the year 1,000 approached.

During the tenth century, we find many nobles in Europe converted
and entering the monasteries. Their influence on medieval life and
civilisation was very marked.

The Eleventh Century – Crusade

Important dates	
1009	Destruction of the Church of the Holy Sepulchre at Jerusalem
1049	Leo IX begins to reform the Church
1054	Rome and Constantinople part over the 'filioque'
1093	Anselm becomes archbishop of Canterbury
1095	Beginning of the Crusades

The tenth century had been a barren period as far as biblical scholarship was concerned. But from the turn of the eleventh century, from the year 1000 onwards, this was to change. Within the church, particularly throughout monastic centres of learning, a new interest in biblical exegesis and exposition developed, and some scholars of note appeared on the scene. Gerald Bray mentions the following:

- Fulbert of Chartres (c.960-1059) wrote a running commentary on the text of the Bible. His school at Chartres attracted biblical scholars. He also rebuilt the cathedral at Chartres after it was destroyed by fire.

- Bruno of Wurzburg (c.1005-45) was an Austrian, of royal descent, and became Bishop of Wurzburg. He wrote a commentary on the Psalms.

- Peter Damian (c.1007-72) was one of the 'reformers' of the period. He used Scripture as a means for reforming and reshaping church life (his interpretation of Scripture was highly allegorical). He was also a strong supporter of priestly celibacy, and wrote attacking what he saw as moral decadence among ministers.

- Bruno the Carthusian (c.1032-1101) was founder of the Carthusian Order. He wrote a commentary on the Psalms and on Paul, again highly allegorical.

One of the significant features of biblical studies in the eleventh century was the development of the *gloss*. This was a method of interpreting the Bible and writing the interpretation in the margin. It probably began with scholars writing short notes in the margin of the text, but these developed into lengthier passages, so that in some editions of the Bible, the text of Scripture appeared on the left and the 'gloss' or interpretation as a parallel column on the right. The glosses were intended to explain the meaning of the text, but often came to include theological questions and discussions in their own right. The study of the glosses has become an important feature of historical studies, as they shed light for us on the kind of biblical interpretation which was going on at the time. The scholars of the medieval church were responsible for preserving much of the earlier interpretation, and were generally very heavily dependent on an allegorical method of interpretation. There also seems to be some evidence for the use of chapter divisions in the biblical text at this time.

The Papacy in the eleventh century
This period was a period of important developments as far as the papacy and the power of the Roman Church were concerned. At one point in the century, from 1044-1046, three different men each claimed to be the pope – Benedict IX, Silvester III, and Gregory VI. This reflected the power struggles of different parties and factions in Rome, each claiming to have the authority to settle their own candidate in the papal office. The consequent confusion and instability resulted in a synod being convened in 1046, called by the Emperor Henry III. Silvester and Benedict were deposed, while Gregory was banished. One historian calls this 'the highwater mark of imperial control over the papacy'.[79] The emperor nominated the next popes: Clement II, who was pontiff in 1046-7, Damasus II, who reigned for a few days, and then Leo IX (1049-1054).

These were truly dark days as far as the church of Christ was concerned, yet Leo IX saw the reform of the church as one of his primary concerns. In a sense he laid the foundation for the Catholic Church of the future. The controversy over the appointment of popes led to him ensuring that responsibility for papal elections would rest solely with the college of cardinals, the leading bishops of the church who became the pope's advisers in Rome. When Leo became pope, the cardinals were Roman bishops, and the authority of the Church was very much centralised in Rome. He changed this, so that the whole of the Western Church was represented in the cardinalate.

Three of the new cardinals appointed by Leo were to have great influence in the history of the church. Humbert of Lorraine was a monk who had a strong influence over the political interests of the pope. Hugh the White, another French monk, was a long-standing supporter of reform. But one of the important names of the eleventh century was Hildebrand of Germany (c.1020-85), who was to become Pope Gregory VII. He had accompanied Leo from Germany when Leo became pope, and he was immediately given the responsibility of the finances of the Roman See. He has been described as 'the most remarkable personality in medieval papal history. A man of diminutive stature and unimpressive appearance, his power of intellect, firmness of will and limitlessness of design made him the outstanding figure of his age.'[80]

Hildebrand had been educated within a monastery of the Cluny order in Rome. When Gregory was banished to Germany, he went with him, and then returned with Leo, championing the cause of reform in the church. Hildebrand himself eventually became pope in 1073.

Leo determined to raise the status of the Papacy. To achieve this, he called a series of synods in different places throughout the empire. In 1049 he condemned both simony (the practice of offering ecclesiastical benefits for money) and priestly marriage. While he strengthened the cause of the church in the West, he was responsible for the formal separation of the Western Church from the Greek Orthodox Church of the East by excommunicating Michael Cerularius, the Patriarch of Constantinople, over the 'filioque' issue. Leo's action is significant as marking the break between the two wings of the church. Leo was captured in a battle against the Normans in 1054, and he died a broken man the following year.

A succession of popes followed, but Gregory VII is regarded as the adviser and the architect of papal power during this period. At a Roman synod of 1059, an important decision was taken to ensure that popes were chosen by the cardinals rather than by the emperor. This synod produced one of the earliest constitutional documents on which the modern Roman Catholic Church is based. This was to ensure that the choice of pope would remain within the church and would be independent of political interference. The synod also marked a formal break between papacy and empire. The eleventh century thus marks a move towards the complete independence of Rome and the power of the pope, largely driven by Gregory VII's determination 'to make the Roman See the effective law-making and law-enforcing authority in Western Christendom'.[81]

In spite of the reforms that were undertaken to rid the church of worldliness and to leave it independent of the political intrigues of the time, there were clear breaches of biblical teaching and practice going on. One of these was the system of indulgences, with the pope assuming the power to grant pardon of sins on the basis of a payment of some kind. It was argued that since one drop of Christ's blood would have been sufficient to atone for the sins of the whole race, the fulness of Christ's sacrifice has yielded a treasure, committed by God to Peter and his successors, 'to be used for the full or partial remission of the sins of the faithful who have repented and confessed'.[82] It was not long before this came to be applied to the dead, allegedly to release them from purgatory. Despite the requirement for confession, indulgences came to be seen as a shortcut to forgiveness and salvation.

The Crusades

One of the features of the late eleventh century was the beginning of the Crusades. These 'holy wars' were ostensibly for the re-control of Jerusalem and other places from the Muslims who controlled and occupied them, but then became an excuse for the church to embark on any kind of armed campaign. The system of indulgences was linked to the success of the Crusades, because Pope Urban II, who encouraged the first Crusade in 1095, promised complete pardon to those who would take part. A.M. Renwick reckons that 'the Crusades did more to popularize Indulgences than any other single movement'.[83]

In 1009, the Church of the Holy Sepulchre in Jerusalem was

destroyed, and Muslim occupation of the holy city was a source of grief to the Roman Church. The pope encouraged the crusades in order to recapture these holy places from Muslim control, but also as a means of consolidating the power of the Papacy itself. He persuaded the people to join the crusades by firing their imagination, and at a council at Clermont (France) in 1095 he summoned them 'to take up the cross to liberate the Holy Land from Islam. Princes and nobles were moved by the prospect of a war which not merely gave the promise of loot and adventure but of spiritual reward. The crusading army captured Jerusalem, set up a Christian feudal kingdom and restored papal control over the holy places, for a Latin patriarch was enthroned in Jerusalem'.[84]

Renwick estimates that some 300,000 people joined this first Crusade, expecting that God would provide miraculously for them. The result was that many of them perished either of cold, or hunger, or both, and most through inexperience. The alleged Christian spirit of the Crusades was belied when the surviving rump reached Jerusalem and immediately began to pillage, plunder and massacre the Muslim occupants of the holy city. The Crusaders left Clermont in 1095, captured Nicaea in 1097, Antioch in 1098 and Jerusalem in 1099.

It is important to grasp the mixed motives which stirred over a quarter of a million people to march under the Christian banner against Muslim Jerusalem:

> Love of adventure, hopes for plunder, desire for territorial advancement and religious hatred, undoubtedly moved the Crusaders with very earthly impulses. We should wrong them, however, if we did not recognize with equal clearness that they thought they were doing something of the highest importance for their souls and for Christ.[85]

That is no excuse, of course, for the atrocities which were carried out, and the Crusades remain a blot on the history of the Christian church.

Anselm

There were several notable Christian leaders whose lives and influence spanned the eleventh and the twelfth centuries.

Anselm (1033-1109) was archbishop of Canterbury from 1093 to 1109. He had become a monk in 1060 and had become prior of Bec, Normandy, in 1063. He was a diligent and reforming archbishop, who encouraged synods and enforced clerical celibacy. Ironically, he was opposed to his own enthronement as archbishop, and prosecuted much of his studies in a monastery in Gaul.

One of Anselm's great principles was that faith and reason are not antithetical. Faith must lead to the proper use of reason. In his *Proslogion*, he expresses it thus: 'I am not seeking to understand in order to believe, but I believe in order to understand. For this too I believe: that unless I believe, I shall not understand'. His philosophy led him to put forward the 'ontological' argument for the existence of God. God, Anselm argued, is 'that than which no greater can be conceived'. This was an attempt to prove the existence of God by the use of reason, and built on Augustine's thought. Although the argument has difficulties, it nonetheless raised a rational defence of Christian theism even in the darkness of the Middle Ages, and continues to be debated by philosophers.

Anselm's greatest work was his *Cur Deus Homo* (*Why God became man*), written in the 1090s. It is a work written in the form of a dialogue and seeks to offer reasons for the incarnation. It was arguably in the doctrine of the atonement that Anselm made his greatest contribution to the development of theology. Anselm argued that Christ made satisfaction for sin and merited salvation for his people. R.A. Finlayson argues that the keywords in Anselm's doctrine of the atonement were 'satisfaction' and 'merit'.[86] The doctrine wrestled with the question of whether it would have been possible for God to have effected atonement apart from the humiliation of Christ? If it was necessary for Christ to become man in order to make atonement, then this necessity must either be in the nature of God or in the nature of sin. Anselm's important contribution to the doctrine of the atonement was that he studied the atonement (and the consequent humiliation of Jesus Christ) as arising out of an intrinsic necessity in God. This laid the foundation for the Reformed doctrine of the atonement. While mercy is optional with God, salvation could not have been secured without God's justice satisfied, his holiness vindicated and his glory advanced.

With Anselm we are introduced to the movement of thought known as *scholasticism*. The term 'scholastics' was used first as a derogatory term by the thinkers of the sixteenth century to describe the thinkers of the Middle Ages, whom they regarded as primitive and reactionary. It has become the word to describe the education of the monastic schools, the learning of the monasteries, with their commitment to expounding the earlier Christian thinkers. The scholastics placed a great deal of emphasis on the role and use of human reason, and although we may feel this to have been a weakness, they were responsible for a revival of interest in the Bible and in theology in the Medieval period.

The Twelfth Century – Learning

Important dates

1116	Peter Abelard at Paris
1148	Second Crusade
1162	Thomas Becket Archbishop of Canterbury
1189	Third Crusade

The development of scholasticism

Following Anselm, other theologians of note, whose lives spanned the closing years of the eleventh century and the opening years of the twelfth, appeared in the Church. Among them were the following:

Peter Abelard (1079-1142) was born in north France, and has been described as 'probably the most brilliant thinker of the 12th century'.[87] He studied philosophy, and became an independent thinker in his own right. While lodging at Notre Dame Cathedral in Paris, he fathered a child to a young woman whom he was tutoring. This was only the first of several tragedies which marred his otherwise useful and brilliant career as a theologian.

In 1122 he produced a famous work entitled *Yes and No* (*Sic et Non*), in which he set forth 158 different theological questions. In it, he set side by side passages from the Bible and from the earlier church fathers which were apparently contradictory. His aim was not to discredit either the Bible or the fathers, but rather to show that with the proper use of reason you could reconcile even apparent discrepancies. His thought contrasts with that of Anselm, who believed that faith precedes and leads to reason; Abelard's view was that nothing was to be believed until it could first be reasoned and understood. This is to introduce doubt as the first step to faith.

With Abelard, we find theology becoming more of a science than a meditation. The weakness of Abelard's thought was the tendency to move away from the objective truths of Scripture to a subjective, rational view; at the same time, however, his was a welcome break from the monotonous darkness of the medieval period. Abelard's work on the Godhead was condemned in 1121 at a Council, and he himself was summoned to appear before a church council in 1140 where he was condemned. An appeal to Rome did not help his case, and he ended up retiring to Cluny where he studied for the last two years of his life.

Bernard of Clairvaux (1090-1153) was another French theologian, born of noble parents, who entered a monastery in 1113. He became abbot of a new monastery at Clairvaux, and was a conscientious and diligent leader of the monastic community there. He was an opponent of Peter Abelard, and gave strong encouragement to the Second Crusade. Although this Crusade was a failure, Bernard had built up a strong reputation as a devout Christian leader, and his popularity carried him through.

Bernard was a brilliant writer, and an attractive preacher. Many of his letters and documents survive, and cover a wide range of issues. His works include treatises on monasticism, *Grace and Freewill* (in which he argues that our good works are both the result of grace and the result of our own free choices), *Consideration* (a work written to Pope Eugenius III, who was a former pupil of his, in which he encouraged him to give time to meditation and reflection, and in which he emphatically opposed papal tyranny), *Loving God, Steps of Humility and Pride,* and *Sermons on the Song of Solomon*, a sermonic treatment of a monk's life. Bernard was also noted as a hymn-writer. The hymn

> Jesus the very thought of thee
> with sweetness fills the breast,
> but sweeter far thy face to see,
> and in thy presence rest

owes its origin to Bernard. Bernard died in 1153, worn out by a life of asceticism and activity.

Peter Lombard (c.1095-1159) was born in northern Italy and studied under Abelard. He was a student at some of the leading French universities and taught at Paris from 1140 onwards. For the last year of his life he was bishop of Paris.

Several of Lombard's sermons, commentaries and letters survive. But the most important surviving work is his *Four Books of Sentences*, which was really the first systematic theology to be produced in this medieval period. Book 1 covers the Trinity, providence and evil, Book 2 deals with creation, grace and sin, Book 3 with the incarnation, redemption and the commandments, and Book 4 with the sacraments and the last things. Lombard deals with the cardinal aspects of theology with reference to the Bible, the church fathers, and Augustine. He quotes 'sentences' from them and discusses the different opinions. His position was that different theological viewpoints could be resolved with the proper use of reason.

In Lombard we find the first systematised doctrine of the sacraments, and the first appearance of seven sacraments. Lombard's list of sacraments was approved at the Council of Florence in 1439, and became the accepted and standard teaching of the Roman Catholic Church. His view was that the sacraments were not only signs of grace, but the effective cause of grace. While this view was questioned by some, the church in 1215 accepted his teaching and the foundation was laid for later official Roman doctrine. Lombard became known as 'Master of the Sentences', and his work became a standard textbook.

Hugh of St Victor (1096-1141) was born in Saxony (Germany), and entered the school of St Victor in Paris. There he became a master, and argued passionately for faith as something certain, which, he said, was 'above opinion and below science'. He became a participant in the sacrament debate; he listed thirty sacraments as opposed to Lombard's seven. Hugo wrote commentaries on the works of early church thinkers, and on the nature of faith. He was a mystic, for whom the goal of spiritual life was to attain a true mystical vision of God. He was one of Lombard's teachers.

Scholasticism therefore shaped the theology of the medieval Roman Church, laying the foundation for its later theology on a basis of faith supplemented by mysticism on the one hand and reason on the other. Although many of those who held such views were fine, self-denying followers of Christ, the ideas they propounded were at heart rationalistic, bowing to the supremacy of man over the claims of th truth of Scripture.

Further Crusades

The twelfth century saw some further crusading. The first Crusade, although barbaric and cruel in some of its treatment of the Muslims in Jerusalem, was the only 'successful' crusade in that it accomplished what it set out to do. The other Crusades left only a legacy of mistrust and of defeat for the Christian Crusaders.

The second Crusade was in 1147-8. The Turks had captured Edessa from the Christians in 1144, and the Second Crusade, inspired by Pope Eugene III and Bernard of Clairvaux, set out to retake Edessa. Part of the failure of this Crusade grew out of a mistrust between the Western Crusaders and the Eastern guides they had employed to help them take Edessa; the Crusader army was decimated, and an attempt to capture Damascus failed miserably.

Later in the twelfth century (1189-92), a third Crusade set out to retake Jerusalem, which had been recaptured in 1187, by Saladin, the leader of the Saracens. The leaders of this third Crusade were Frederick Barbarossa, the Emperor, Philip II of France, and Richard the Lionheart of England. Frederick was drowned during a river crossing, and Philip returned to France. Richard made some gains, but entered into a treaty with Saladin. The whole Crusade was a shambles, and failed to achieve its goal.

Resistance movements

During these centuries of the Medieval period, the church was identified with the Roman Catholic Church of Western Europe. The Papacy had developed into a controlling power over the church, and had assumed a role which was quite out of keeping with the teaching of Scripture. Although not everyone had accepted absolutely everything the Roman church promulgated, there had been no centralised action against voices of dissent.

This changed over the course of the twelfth and thirteenth centuries. With the establishing of a strong Papacy, the church took steps to make sure that any dissident voice or movement would be dealt with. In 1162, Pope Alexander III began measures, ratified by the Lateran Council of 1179, to discover and deal with 'heretics'. This laid the foundation for the Inquisition of the thirteenth century.

Under the good hand of God, the truth of Christ was preserved within certain groups and movements which arose throughout Europe. These groups are still regarded as heretical by some historians, yet we can see in them the beginnings of the movement which would flower in the Reformation of the fifteenth and sixteenth centuries. These were groups of people who believed that the Roman Church had compromised the Word of God and the doctrines of the faith, and that it was necessary either to purify the church or to provide a biblical alternative.

One of the 'resistance movements' was that of the Waldensians. In 1175 Peter Waldo, a wealthy French merchant, became a Christian. He decided to follow Christ's example by leading a life of poverty and preaching. This he saw as being in marked contrast to the affluence of the established Church. Also, in contrast to the Roman Church, he had the New Testament translated into a vernacular tongue, which could easily be understood by all, and he made this the basis of his evangelism. The Archbishop of Lyons prohibited their preaching in 1181, but the Waldensians were spurred on to greater and more zealous witness. Their poverty exposed the worldliness of the clergy. The Pope excommunicated them in 1184, and the movement which had been popular at the beginning, within a decade was branded heretical and was excommunicated.

The Waldensians organised themselves as a church with bishops and priests, and claimed to be the true church. They spread throughout Europe. The story of the Roman Church's reaction to them takes us into the next century.

Another of these movements was the *Cathars* or Albigensians in the south of France. The French peasants objected to the massive wealth the church had gathered for itself, and the oppression represented by the church. The Cathars ('the pure ones') formed a church of their own with ministers and sacraments, criticising some of the excessive claims of the Roman Catholic Church.

The Albigensian movement grew, and by the end of the century the local aristocracy was actively giving them support. The church regarded them as heretical and laboured for their conversion. While some of their viewpoints were undoubtedly heretical, their significance is to be seen in the fact that they raised a standard of opposition against the claims and excesses of the Roman Church of the period.

Developments in the British church

Little is known of the church in the Highlands and Islands during this period. We know that a Synod held in Cashel, in Ireland, in 1172, brought the Celtic church in Ireland fully under the supremacy of Rome. Through the influence of Norway, the Roman church had established the See of Sodor, which included the islands on the west coast of Britain, including the Western Isles to the Isle of Man in the south. In 1188, by a Bull of Pope Clement III, the Scottish church was declared to be under the sovereignty of Rome, and the country was divided into nine Roman dioceses. The Roman church concentrated on establishing itself in various places, such as Inverness-shire, Beauly, and Elgin.

One of the important and famous churchmen of the twelfth century was Thomas Becket (1118-70), Archbishop of Canterbury from 1162 to 1170. He championed the cause of the episcopal church against the interference of the monarch, King Henry II. Henry wished to influence the law as it bore on the lives of churchmen, and also wished to forbid appeals to Rome. Becket stood for the independence of church courts and the right of appeal. As a result he was driven into exile. On his return from exile, he excommunicated several bishops who supported the king, and on 29 December 1170, four of the king's knights entered Canterbury cathedral and murdered Becket at the altar. Society was shocked by this outrage, and a cult developed around the murdered archbishop, who was canonized by the Pope in 1173. Although stout in his allegiance to the Roman authorities, Becket stands out as a man of great courage and strong conscience.

The twelfth century was a period of expansion and consolidation for the Roman Church. Yet it was also a time of opposition, of independent thought and conscientious action. The seeds of reformation were being sown even at this early point.

The Thirteenth Century – Domination

Important dates

1216	Recognition of Dominicans
1226	Death of Francis of Assisi
1232	Roman Inquisition
1274	Death of Thomas Aquinas
1293	Christian missions to China

Responses to resistance

We saw that in the twelfth century some resistance groups sprang up within Europe, particularly the Waldensians and the Cathars. In order to meet the challenges of these groups – which emphasised poverty, asceticism and simple devotion to Christ – new monastic orders sprang up. One of these was the Dominican Order, called after Dominic (c.1170-1221), a native of Calaroga (old Castile). He became a canon, but from about the beginning of the thirteenth century he travelled in the south of France, where he encountered the Cathars. Dominic realised that if the Cathars were to be regained for the Roman Church, the Roman missionaries and priests would have to be just as self-denying and as zealous as the Cathar ministers and preachers themselves.

Dominic took charge of a new monastery in Toulouse, and eventually won papal approval for his new order in 1216. He sent his preachers and missionaries far and wide. In 1216, the Dominican Order was officially licensed by the Pope; its preachers became well-known and soon developed a reputation for devotion to Christ. Dominic himself died in 1221; his order was represented across Europe and in the leading universities of the day.

The reputation of the Dominicans was exceeded only by that of the Franciscans, the order established by Francis of Assisi (c.1181-1226). He was the son of an Italian cloth merchant. Francis pledged himself to the restoration of church buildings which had fallen into ruin and disrepair. In 1208 he had an experience in which he believed the voice of God came to him, calling him to devote himself to a life of poverty and of preaching. He determined to live as Christ had done, imitating him and preaching his message. Some twelve or so companions joined him and Francis drew up a Rule for them. With the approval of the Pope they called themselves the Penitents of Assisi from 1216 onwards.

The Franciscan order was missionary-minded. The Franciscans went around in pairs, preaching wherever they could. In 1219 Francis himself preached before the Sultan of Egypt. Many joined the organisation. He died in 1226, by which time his movement had been domesticated into the Roman Church. There is evidence to suggest that by the time of Francis' death the movement had moved far from his founding ideals. He had relinquished leadership of it in order to live according to his own ideals of ascetism and poverty.

The Dominicans and the Franciscans won a great deal of popular support and influence. Their philosophies were different: the Dominicans emphasised doctrine and learning, while the Franciscans were practical in outlook: they worked mainly in the cities, and strengthened religion among the lower classes (although several later scholars of note, such as Duns Scotus and William of Occam, were Franciscans). Common to both was the practice of mendicancy (begging). There were divisions in the Franciscan Order following Francis' death, between those who valued the poverty and Christ-like spirit of the movement, and those who valued the popularity and the numerical strength of the order. The emphasis on poverty was a threat to the Papacy itself; following Francis' death, some Franciscans were imprisoned.

Further Crusades

The Roman Church continued the Crusades over the course of the thirteenth century. The fourth Crusade was from 1200 to 1204, with the authorisation of Pope Innocent III. The object of it was to undermine the power of the Turks by invading Egypt, but the war became very messy, with the Christian city of Zara and the city of Constantinople being sacked. The fifth Crusade was similar in its aim, and is dated from 1217 to 1221. Part of the goal was achieved – the Crusaders reached Egypt, and took Damietta, but lost it again. A sixth Crusade to regain Jerusalem in 1229 ended with a treaty being made with the Sultan, giving the Emperor Frederick control of Jerusalem, for which he was excommunicated. The last Crusade, aimed at invading the Holy Land via Egypt, led to massive defeat in Egypt in 1254.

As we noted already, the motives of the Crusaders were very mixed. Renwick summarises: 'The immorality, pillage and massacre which so often disgraced the movement show that in spite of great zeal in pursuance of an ideal, no true spiritual power had taken possession of them. The effects were mainly political and social rather than religious.'[88]

The Inquisition

One of the shameful legacies of the thirteenth century was the Inquisition. The aim of this was to combat heresy, but really it was an instrument for ensuring the complete domination of the Roman Catholic Church over all thought and religious enquiry. The architect of the Inquisition was Pope Gregory IX, who appointed an Inquisitor, usually one of the Dominicans (who had the nickname 'the Lord's watchdogs'), to search out those who were suspected of being heretics, and to get them to confess. They were given a defence counsel, but this was a sham, for the evidence was weighted against them. Pope Innocent IV issued a Bull in 1252 which allowed the Inquisitor to use torture to break the will of the alleged heretics. It was a heinous system which was intended to bring into submission any who dared question the received wisdom of the Roman Church. The medieval Inquisition is to be distinguished from the more barbaric Spanish Inquisition of the fifteenth century. In many independent-minded countries, this papal interference was much resented, and in 1252 the Inquisitor Peter Martyr was assassinated.

The development of scholasticism

Anselm had laid the foundation of a new movement of thought in the Middle Ages that sought to recover the primacy of faith as the first step in philosophical enquiry. He had been followed by others in the twelfth century. Scholastic thought continued to be at the forefront of theological enquiry during the thirteenth century. The following names are prominent:

John Bonaventure (1221-74) was born in Tuscany. He became a Franciscan at the age of seventeen, soon becoming the head of the Franciscan Order. He also taught theology as a professor in Paris. He wrote a life of St Francis, a work on the Poverty of Christ, and a work entitled *Journey of the Mind to God*. He believed that true knowledge can only come through contemplation of God. God is different from man in quality and in quantity, and can be experienced by man only through deep and serious reflection. Bonaventure became a bishop in 1273, and left a legacy of many biblical commentaries.

John Duns Scotus (1265-1308) is regarded as one of the great scholastic theologians of the medieval period. He was educated and taught at Oxford before coming to Paris. Scotus' theology built on the premise that the essence of God is will. God's will is free; the individual is the supreme thing. Scotus argued that the atonement is effective not because it was necessary, but because God willed it. He minimised the importance of repentance and confession: it is enough that God wills to forgive. Duns Scotus was one of the first theologians to defend the doctrine of the Immaculate Conception.

One of the most important names of the period is that of Thomas Aquinas (1225-74). Aquinas was born to a noble family in Aquino (between Rome and Naples). He entered the Dominican Order in 1243, and during the mid-thirteenth century he developed a strong intellectual ability which brought scholasticism to its height. He borrowed heavily from Aristotle and Augustine. His two most important works were his *Summa Theologiae*, an extensive summary of Christian doctrine,[89] and his *Summa Contra Gentiles*, a rational explanation for Christian faith. Although some took issue with Aquinas, the Council of Trent (1545-63) adopted his work as the basis of Roman Catholic dogma, and in 1879 the Pope declared that Thomism (the theology of Aquinas) was valid for all time.

In the *Summa Theologiae*, Aquinas summarises the five ways philosophers have proved the existence of God. Together, these have been regarded as affording strong rational proof that God exists. Aquinas argued for the existence of God:

1. From the changes that occur in the world: everything is in a state of change, and everything is changed by something else. There must be something, or someone who is the originator of all change and yet remains unchanged. This we call God.

2. From the nature of causation: everything in the world has a cause. Nothing pre-exists. It is brought into being. Without an underived primary cause, you would have nothing at all. God is therefore the First Cause of all things.

3. From the nature of necessity: there are some things which are unnecessary. Because they are unnecessary they last only for a short while. Just because a thing is capable of existing, doesn't mean it has necessarily to exist. There must be something which necessarily exists, and which gives existence to everything else, and which needs nothing else. This we call God.

4. From the comparison of virtues. It was similar to the argument of Anselm, that God is the superlative being. The greatest, the loveliest, the best, the most perfect imaginable is what we call God.

5. From the order in nature. If things work out towards a goal, it must be because there is design. God is the supreme designer.

These five ways are not without philosophical difficulty, and are still debated. But unlike Scotus, who grounded the existence of God in the exercise of God's will, Aquinas grounded the existence of God in the simple fact of God's being. God is the absolute being, and the source of all things.

Aquinas laid the foundation for much Roman Catholic doctrine. In his view of the atonement he combined the view of Anselm that emphasised satisfaction, and that of Abelard, which emphasised moral example, and taught that salvation was an additional gift (in addition to the natural virtues of men) by which God's favour could be won with Christ's merit. Grace is channelled through the sacraments alone; Aquinas accepted Lombard's list of seven sacraments.

Study of Thomistic thought occupies scholarly discussion still. The most interesting aspect of this was the rivalry between the thought of Scotus (the Scotist school) and that of Aquinas (the Thomist school).

It was more than a rivalry between Dominicans and Fransiscans; it was the rivalry between two opposing philosophical tendencies and heralded the breakdown of scholasticism, because it failed to show the reasonableness of Christianity. It only demonstrated that rational argument must not be our starting-point. Aquinas' theology became popularised in the work of Dante Alighieri, the great medieval poet, whose *Divine Comedy* reflects Roman Catholic (and specifically Franciscan) influence.

The Fourteenth Century – Schism

Important dates	
1309-72	The Avignonese Captivity of the Papacy
1327-47	Labours of William of Occam
1378	Beginning of the Great Schism of the Papacy
1384	Death of John Wycliffe

By the beginning of the fourteenth century the Roman Church had spread far and wide, and the Pope had consolidated his authority by various means. Pope Boniface VIII declared that the year 1300 should be a jubilee, or holy year, and encouraged pilgrimages to Rome. Pilgrims were enticed with the promise of obtaining indulgences and forgiveness. In 1302, he issued a Papal Bull – the *Unam Sanctam* – which asserted that the Pope had universal jurisdiction. But this high watermark was short-lived, as we shall see, and by the end of the century the Papacy was embroiled in a bitter controversy.

The fourteenth century also saw the end of scholasticism. The great figures of this rationalistic movement had flourished in the previous century; one of the last of the Schoolmen worthy of note was William of Occam (c.1285-1347). He was a native of Surrey. He entered the Franciscan Order and studied under John Duns Scotus. He ministered in England, Paris and Munich, and was excommunicated for his pains. He denied that the church had any authority in civil matters, and also opposed the infallibility of the Pope.

Occam believed that theological doctrines are to be received on authority; they are not philosophically demonstrable. He wished to assert that the authority of the Church was the basis for accepting theological truth, although his controversy with the Pope made this unworkable, and he did end up asserting that Scripture alone has authority over the mind of the believer. In contrast to the controversies raised in the scholastic theology of Aquinas and Scotus, Occam was

117

asserting a new, modern, middle way, which held sway until the Reformation. But it lacked a robust defence of Christian doctrine. Occam was a deep thinker, and a thorough rationalist, who was noted for sorting out the essential points of an argument and getting to the crux of the matter quickly. His basic philosophical position was that we can have direct experience of things, a view which is known as "nominalism". The phrase "Occam's razor" is used to describe the way he 'shaved off' all the unnecessary points of an argument, so as to proceed with as few assumptions as possible. Martin Luther would later claim that he was in this philosophical stream.

The spread of the church

By 1300 the first Roman Catholic missionaries had reached China. A church had been established in Peking in 1291, which flourished for a time. During the course of the fourteenth century, the church in China was established with bishops and priests, and continued to grow until the Ming dynasty expelled foreigners in 1368.

In the early years of the fourteenth century there was an effort at missionary training. A famous native of Majorca, Ramon Lull (died 1315) was burdened for the educated Muslims, whom he wished to win over to Christianity. He wrote a defence of the Christian faith for this purpose, and laboured extensively in Tunis and in Africa. He was martyred in 1315, having achieved little, but having fuelled the fires of missionary endeavour.

Neither the Crusades nor the missionary work of the church, however, could prevent the loss of Palestine to the Muslims. The Ottoman Turks invaded Europe in the mid-fourteenth century and by the time of the Reformation they had invaded half of Europe. The period, therefore, was marked by the loss of territories that were once Christian.

Opposition to the church

In the thirteenth century the main opposition to the teachings of the Roman Catholic Church was from the Waldensians and from the Cathars in France. More opposition grew in the fourteenth century, from men who were the forerunners of the Reformation.

Thomas Bradwardine (1290-1349) was an English mathematician

and theologian who became Archbishop of Canterbury. He emphasised the priority and primacy of grace in the salvation of sinners. He was responsible for encouraging the study of Augustine's theology. He taught theology at Oxford, and was influential in spreading a pre-Reformation Augustinian tradition.

Gregory of Rimini (died 1358) was an Italian philosopher who became a monk and also studied and preached Augustinian theology. He emphasised the grace of God in salvation and also taught the doctrine of predestination, laying the foundation for later Calvinistic doctrine.

One of the most famous names of the fourteenth century was that of John Wycliffe (1329-84), who has been called the morning star of the Reformation. Wycliffe was a native of Yorkshire who studied in Oxford. In 1374 he became rector of Lutterworth, and that same year he was appointed a delegate to meet with representatives of the Pope over a dispute. By 1376 Wycliffe had become disenchanted with the church's accumulation of wealth and the sale of indulgences. He had also come to deny transubstantiation as a biblical doctrine, emphasising the authority of the Bible in all matters of faith and life. In 1377 he was called to answer for his new views before the bishop of London, and the Pope had ordered his arrest and examination.

He did, however, have popular support, and continued his work in lecturing and writing. He taught that the church is not the college of cardinals and the Pope, but the whole body of God's elect. His most enduring legacy was the translation of the Bible from the Latin Vulgate into the English tongue. This was done between 1382 and 1384, with a revision in 1388. It is not known how much of the project Wycliffe himself carried out, but it is thought that the New Testament was largely his work. The translation was made from the Latin, and not from the original, and was a word-for-word translation, and therefore to some extent unreadable. It was not printed until the nineteenth century; the original copies were written by hand and proved expensive. His principle was that 'Christ and his apostles taught the people in the tongue that was best known to the people. Why should not men do so now?' Wycliffe's abiding contribution to the work of the church is the production of the first English translation of the Bible, and it was the Bible that was to light the flame of Reformation zeal and piety.

The next step in Wycliffe's reforming work was to bring the Bible to the people, through evangelism and mission. The preachers whom he sent out were the Lollards, known as the 'poor preachers' or the 'Bible men'. Their principle was that of *sola scriptura* – the Bible alone – and from that base they attacked much of contemporary church life and practice. They endured persecution for their faith, but remained courageous and undaunted in their efforts to reach men with the gospel.

Wycliffe died in his parish of Lutterworth in 1384. However, in 1428, in response to the Roman Church's condemnation of his teaching and work, his body was exhumed, burned, and his remains cast into the River Swift. It was an ignoble and unfitting end for a man whose work and labours precipitated the movement of the Reformation.

No less significant was the work of John Hus (c.1370-1415). He was a Bohemian priest who was a professor of theology at the University of Prague. He too opposed the sale of indulgences and the veneration of images, and defined the church in terms of Christlike living, rather than in terms of the sacraments. Hus had been born a poor peasant, but became a powerful preacher of the gospel whose preaching threatened the luxury of the Roman clerics. He was excommunicated in 1411, after defying a ban on his preaching. The Council of Constance treated him shamefully and ordered him to be burnt at the stake in 1415.

Papal difficulties

Although the fourteenth century had opened with the Pope in a position of supreme power, things were to change swiftly for the Roman Church. Two tragedies befell the Papacy during the fourteenth century.

The first is known as the *Avignonese Captivity*. This was a period from 1309 to 1372 in which the Popes resided outside Italy, a period of seventy years which some historians have compared to the Babylonian Captivity of the Old Testament era. When Clement V, a weak and immoral character, became Pope in 1305, he was under the influence of King Philip IV of France. The French domination of the Papacy was signalled by the removal of the Pope to Avignon in 1309. This was a major weakening of Papal power, and was the first time that the Pope resided outside of Rome.

The significance of this is striking. It showed, first, that the Pope regarded himself as less of a religious figure and more a secular figure; one historian describe the move to Avignon as the 'bureaucratization of the papacy'.[90] Vivian Green goes on: 'the Pope himself came more and more to have the attributes and trappings of a secular prince, both as the ruler of the papal state and through his interference in politics, disguised as matters of religious moment.'[91] It meant, secondly, that the prestige of the Pope suffered. If the head of the church could so easily be swayed under the power of a secular monarch, then moral and religious authority would suffer. It meant that mission and evangelism were severely weakened. And it also meant that any authority that the Pope had became more and more centralised in his person rather than in the ruling body which regulated the church. Also, in order to maintain the high luxurious standards of the papacy, the church was heavily taxed, which did not endear the papal office to the majority of the people. The Avignonese papacy of these years served to weaken the papal institution.

The second weakening of the Papacy followed the Avignonese Captivity. In 1378, Pope Gregory XI died. During the Captivity, all the Popes had been French, which did not help the politics of the day, especially since England was at war with France for most of this time. Gregory XI was urged by St Catherine of Sienna to return the papacy to its rightful seat in Rome, which he did, but then he died suddenly the following year. By this time, most of the cardinals were French, and would have returned to Avignon, but the Roman people wished to retain the papacy in Italy. The result was that the cardinals elected Pope Urban VI as Pope, but he was a tactless man who turned the cardinals against him. They decided, four months later, to declare their election of him void, and chose Clement VII who fought for three years with Urban VI, after which he moved to Avignon. So now there were two popes: Urban VI in Rome, and Clement VII in Avignon. This was the beginning of what is called The Great Schism of the Papacy (1378-1417).

In Rome, Urban VI was followed by Boniface IX, Innocent VII and Gregory XII. In Avignon, Clement VII was followed by Benedict XIII. Both streams claimed to be the true papacy. Europe was divided. Germany, Norway and England declared their support of the Roman pontiff. Scotland, France and Spain followed the Avignon Pope. The two Popes maintained their luxurious lifestyle, both lording it over the people. But the most devastating consequence was that two Popes threatened the doctrine of the unity of the Church.

In order to try to bring some order into this chaos, the cardinals of both Popes got together and convened a Council at Pisa in 1409. Neither Pope attended, and the Council declared both Popes deposed. As Walker points out, this was in itself a bold move, because it was an assertion 'that the council was superior to the papacy'.[92] Both Popes refused to step down and were deposed by a second Council at Constance in 1415. Meanwhile the Council of Pisa had appointed Alexander V as Pope, so that from 1409 there were three men all claiming to be the true successors of St Peter.

It was in 1417, with the appointment of Martin V as Pope that order and unity were restored at a third Council at Constance. But the interesting outcome of all of this was that 'it secured the transformation of the papacy from an absolute into a constitutional monarchy. The Pope was to remain the executive of the church, but was to be regulated by a legislative body, meeting at frequent intervals and representing all interests in Christendom.'[93]

The Avignonese Captivity and the Great Schism had done great damage to the Roman Church in general and to the Papal office in particular, and was another symptom of the crying need in Europe for a complete Reformation of the church.

The Fifteenth Century – Dawn

Important dates

1415	Death of John Hus
1418	Publication of Thomas à Kempis' influential *Imitation of Christ*
1479	Establishing of the Spanish Inquisition
1483	Birth of Martin Luther

The religious scene

Around 1418, the *Imitation of Christ* by Thomas à Kempis (1380-1471) was published. Thomas spent most of his long life in a monastery. His *Imitation* has been called 'the choicest devotional handbook of the Middle Ages',[94] and is divided into four parts: Some thoughts to help with the spiritual life; Some advice on the inner life; Spiritual comfort; and A recommendation to holy communion. It has appeared in many editions.

This devotional emphasis is a reminder to us of the fact that the intellectual pursuits of the schoolmen were not enough to satisfy the total needs of the church. There is need for a robust defence and explanation of the faith; but there is also need for the devotional life of the soul to be nurtured. The one requires the other for healthy spirituality. The danger in the MiddleAges was that these were being separated from one another, with the schoolmen emphasising doctrine, and the mystics emphasising devotion.

Amid this state of affairs was the Papacy, which was in a state of decline. 'Its desire was to consolidate and increase the States [i.e. possessions of land] of the Church and maintain political independence. Its ambitions and its aims were like those of other Italian rulers. The papacy became secularized as at no other period in its history.'[95] The fifteenth-century popes were embroiled in political wranglings, and became notorious in seeking wealth for themselves and others. It was rumoured that many priests and popes had fathered children, and were advancing their status and wealth by an abuse of papal power.

There was also great ecclesiastical opposition to Wycliffe's Bible, which, as we saw, was the first main attempt to translate the Scriptures into the language of the people. After his death, his secretary, John Purvey, revised his translation, and published it with a prologue and notes. But the church issued a decree in 1408, known as the Constitutions of Oxford, which forbade people to translate or read any of the Bible in the vernacular language without the approval of a bishop or church council. Purvey and others were imprisoned for their efforts to make the Word of God known. But a desire for the Bible continued and there was obvious need for the Scriptures to be distributed.

This was a great era in the history of the world, 'the age of navigation and geographical discoveries.'[96] Gutenburg, who invented printing, brought out a Latin Psalter in 1457, the first dated printed Scripture. Three years later in 1460 the Gutenberg Bible, a printed version of the Latin Vulgate, was published.

The development of humanism

In this flowering of culture and of thought, a movement known as humanism grew. We usually use the term 'humanism' to mean an anti-theistic philosophical movement. But sixteenth-century humanism was really the development of an anti-ecclesiastical movement, which was aware of the corruptions in the Roman Church and of the anti-intellectualism of the established religion. This new humanism was an attempt to get people to think for themselves, and there is a sense in which the Reformation grew out of it. Calvinism is nothing if it is not an attempt to allow people to think for themselves. The Reformers were humanists in the best sense of the term.

Lorenzo Valla (1407-57) was one of the leaders of the humanistic movement. His main problem was with the claims of the Pope to temporal sovereignty. He also challenged the church by insisting that it was not enough to read the Latin Vulgate – it was necessary to get back to the original Scriptures. This was too independent a mind-set for the church to entertain.

Johann Eck (1486-1543) was a man of great learning, and became professor of theology in 1510. For a time he was a supporter of Martin Luther but following a quarrel between them, Eck led a Catholic reaction to Luther, and contributed to Luther's being excommunicated in 1520. He wrote in defence of indulgences, and produced a version of the Bible in German dialect for the use of the Roman Catholic believers.

One of the greatest of these humanists was Desiderius Erasmus of Rotterdam (1466-1536), highly regarded and reputedly the greatest thinker of his age. He was an opponent of monasticism and an intellectual critic of scholasticism. He was responsible for a renewed interest in the classics and of textual criticism. Following a spell of teaching at Cambridge, Erasmus returned to Basel, where he produced an edition of the Greek New Testament which challenged the Vulgate of Jerome. Erasmus' thought and teaching sat well neither with the Roman Catholic nor with the Reformed scholars, and was often reviled on both sides.

Humanism was an intellectual movement which developed alongside the contemporary Renaissance of the time. It was a period when the arts and culture flourished; in Europe over two dozen universities were founded in the early fifteenth century. There was a new confidence in the power of human culture and intellect, a reaction to both the arid scholasticism and the introspective and self-assured church culture of the period. The humanists advocated a return to the sources. Erasmus was one of several who applied this to Christian theology and dogma, advocating that tradition was not enough; the church needed to get back to its sources, to the Bible in the original and to the simplicity of the church fathers. Despite its name, therefore, humanism played an important role in the Reformation, which, in its purest sense, called the church back to its foundational documents.

Precursors of the Reformation

Several faithful servants of Christ were raised up in this era in which Reformation light was beginning to dawn and to shine on the church. Many of the Reformers were born in the closing years of the fifteenth century and flourished in the next.

One of the fifteenth century reformers was Girolamo Savonarola (1452-98). He was an Italian preacher of reform who had studied humanism and medicine before becoming a monk in the Dominican order. He was a popular preacher and rose to a position of prominence in the government of Florence. Having effected a reform of the civil corruptions of Florence, he denounced the papacy and was excommunicated. The Pope used his power to frighten the citizens of Florence into executing Savonarola, who became a hero to the early Protestant movement.

In England, one of the most influential men was John Colet (1466-1519), who worked in Oxford and broke away from the humanism of the schoolmen. His Oxford lectures on the Pauline epistles brought them to life for many people. He preached a sermon in Oxford in 1512 in which he denounced the excesses of the church and declared that with the reform of the bishops, the whole church would be reformed. Erasmus and Tyndale both came under his influence.

William Tyndale (1494-c.1536) was influential in the sixteenth century and was put to death for his reforming zeal. His influence was in the area of Bible publication and translation, and he deserves to be recognised as a precursor of the Reformation movement. Tyndale set out to make an English translation of the Bible from the original. He discovered that there was no place in the whole of England where he could get his work done, so went to the Continent and published his first version of the English Bible in 1517. The Authorised Version reproduces about ninety per cent of Tyndale's Bible, which shows how thoroughly he did his work, and how influential his work became. Tyndale's prayer when put to death at the stake was that God would open the king of England's eyes, and there is no doubt that the wide availability of the Bible played a large part in the development of the Reformation movement.

The Sixteenth Century – Reform

Important dates	
1514	Birth of John Knox
1516	Publication of Erasmus' New Testament
1517	Luther posts his 95 theses on the door of the Wittenberg Church
1521	Teachings of Luther outlawed by the Diet of Worms
1533	Thomas Cranmer becomes Archbishop of Canterbury
1536	Publication of first edition of Calvin's *Institutes*
1560	Scotland adopts Knox's Confession, repudiating Roman supremacy

I want to insert a personal note at this point. One of the most moving experiences of my life was to stand before the Reformation monument in Geneva in the Summer of 1999. A long wall has carved on it some figures depicting the Reformation, and four huge images of the principal Reformers. Much as the artwork attracted me and caused me much thought, the inscription on the wall was equally moving. In large Latin letters there are inscribed the words 'POST TENEBRAS LUX' – 'after darkness, light.' It summarises the whole ethos of the sixteenth century. After darkness, light was about to dawn.

The sixteenth century is predominantly the century of Reformation, in which the church was shaken to its very foundations and re-formed into a more biblical, Christ-centred and God-glorifying body. Reformation history and theology have spawned a massive amount of literature; consequently, unlike some of the other centuries we have studied, the difficulty here is in knowing what to omit.

There is a divergence of opinion concerning the Reformation in scholarly studies about the sixteenth century. Some scholars regard the Protestant Reformation as an unnecessary and unfortunate movement, which split the church and left Christendom worse afterwards. For other scholars, a thoroughgoing Reformation was

The Major Reformers

Martin Luther (1483-1546)
Born in Eisleben, Germany; educated in Leipzig. He entered the priesthood in 1507. Wrote the 95 Theses, which were posted to the church door of Wittenberg in 1517. He was excommunicated in 1520 and called to attend the Diet of Worms in 1521. Married Katherine von Bora in 1525. His works include *The Babylonian Captivity of the Church* and *The Bondage of the Will*.

Ulrich Zwingli (1484-1531)
Born in Toggenburg, Switzerland. Entered the priesthood in 1506. Called to Zurich in 1518. Some of his followers were involved in the Anabaptist movement, and he was instrumental in persecuting them. He was killed in battle. His works include *Sixty-seven Conclusions*.

John Calvin (1509-1564)
Born in Noyon, France, and studied in Paris. It was there he embraced the Protestant faith. Guillaume Farel persuaded him to come to Geneva in 1536 to help the Reformation movement there, but he was forced to leave and went to live in Strasbourg, where he married. He became the leader of the Reformation on his return to Geneva in 1541 and his influence spread from there throughout Europe. His works include the magisterial *Institutes of the Christian Religion*, and commentaries on many books of Scripture.

John Knox (1514-1572)
Born in Haddington, Scotland. He entered the priesthood in 1536. Because of his views he spent some time as a galley slave. He came under Calvin's influence in 1553. Returning to Scotland in 1559, he led the Reformation there. He wrote *The First Blast of the Trumpet Against the Monstrous Regiment of Women* and *History of the Reformation of Religion within the Realm of Scotland*. Knox was also influential in the production of the *Scots Confession* of 1560.

the only way in which the church could get back to its roots. There is no doubt that the Reformation was a movement of the Spirit of God, which was to leave behind a legacy rich in biblical content and in orthodox teaching for subsequent generations.

Even in our enthusiasm about the Reformation, however, we must always remember that there was a church, and a testimony to biblical truth in the pre-reformation era. It was not with Calvin that the truth came into Europe. Even with all its faults, traditions, ceremonies and rituals, there was a witness to the gospel of Jesus Christ within the Roman Catholic Church. This ought to colour our attitude both to the Reformation and to the Roman Catholic Church of our own day. We must also remember that although the Reformation formally began in 1517, it would not have been possible without the contribution of some of the pre-Reformation men whom we have looked at. They laid the foundation on which others built; in particular, they were responsible (a) for the translation and publication of the Scriptures which, more than anything else, precipitated the Reformation movement, and (b) issued a scholarly call to get back to the sources, to the fundamental documents, which, in the case of the church, of necessity meant the Greek and Hebrew Scriptures. This led to a scholarly challenge to the Latin Vulgate, and to the accepted teaching of the Roman Catholic Church.

The Reformation – beginnings

Martin Luther was a German, born in 1483, who was educated at Erfurt. In 1505 he entered an Augustinian monastery, and three years later commenced a teaching career at the University of Wittenberg. On 31 October 1517 he posted 95 theses on the door of the Castle Church in Wittenberg. The particular point of church practice which disturbed him was the sale of indulgences, based on the Pope's claim to be able to shut the gates of Hell and open the door to Paradise. The 95 theses were an invitation to the church leaders to discuss indulgences and related doctrines.

As a result of his study of the Scriptures, particularly the letter to the Romans, Luther came to understand the nature of the righteousness of God. Luther said:

I greatly longed to understand Paul's Epistle to the Romans, and nothing stood in the way but that one expression 'the righteousness of God', because I took it to mean the righteousness whereby God is righteous and deals righteously in punishing the unrighteous.... Night and day I pondered until...I grasped the truth that the righteousness of God is that righteousness whereby, through grace and sheer mercy, he justifies us by faith. Thereupon I felt myself to be reborn and to have gone through open doors into paradise. The whole of Scripture took on a new meaning, and whereas before 'the righteousness of God' had filled me with hate, now it became to me inexpressibly sweet in greater love.

Luther came to see that a theology based on tradition was unsafe and illusory, and that consequently the biblical doctrine of justification by faith alone was the only foundation for the gospel and for real hope. This contrasted greatly with the pretences of the Pope and the church councils of the time.

In December 1517, Luther's stand was brought to the attention of Rome. In disputations during the following years, Luther's stand for the truth of the gospel became even clearer and more public. He was excommunicated in 1520, and was summoned before the Diet of Worms in 1521. He later wrote, 'If I had heard that as many devils would set on me in Worms as there are tiles on the roof, I should none the less have ridden there.' It was at Worms that Luther said, 'Here I stand, I can do no other, so help me God.'

Luther's later work involved him in the publication of the Bible in German, a task which occupied him from 1521 to 1534. The New Testament was completed early in 1522, with the Old Testament occupying him for the next decade or so. Every subsequent version of the German Scriptures was dependent on Luther's translation. Among his publications were *The Bondage of the Will, Catechisms, Lectures on Romans* and *Lectures on Galatians*. Luther's appeal is to the final authority of 'a self-interpreted Bible',[97] and his view of the church is as a priesthood of all believers. The Lutherans developed their own traditions separately from the Reformed churches. The break was not complete in Luther's own day, but occurred in 1580 when the Lutherans issued their mandatory Book of Concord which deliberately ruled out a Reformed understanding of the Lord's Supper and other issues. Though we would question whether everything in Lutheranism is scriptural, the work of Luther was fundamental for the Reformation. He died in 1546.

Incidentally, the story of Luther's life is a clear illustration for us of the fact that the Reformation began within the Roman Church. It was not an imposition from outside, but a transformation from inside.

The Reformation – developments

Around the same time, Ulrich Zwingli (1484-1531) was engaged in reforming work in Switzerland. Zwingli entered the priesthood in order to have a respectable career. He became learned in the biblical languages and the theology of the early church fathers. He was a Swiss army chaplain. Zwingli came under the influence of Erasmus, and while a priest he developed evangelical views. In Zurich he began to lecture on the New Testament and engaged the Catholic bishop in debate.

Zwingli and Luther differed in their views on the Lord's Supper. While Luther argued for a real presence of Christ's body, Zwingli insisted on the doctrine of a spiritual presence. This difference was sharp and it alienated some of the Reformers from each other. Some of Zwingli's opponents broke away to form the Anabaptist movement (that is, those who believed that infant baptism – particularly Roman Catholic baptism – was invalid, and that subsequent adult baptism was required). Zwingli opposed the Anabaptists to the point of persecuting them. He believed in taking up arms in a righteous cause and died in a battle against the Catholics.

In Strasbourg, Martin Bucer (1491-1551) exercised a fruitful ministry of reform. Bucer became known as the Peacemaker of the Reformation, because he tried (unsuccessfully) to mediate between Luther and Zwingli. He had been a Dominican monk who also came under Erasmus' spell. Bucer lectured at Cambridge in his final years, where he and Thomas Cranmer met and discussed various aspects of the faith. Bucer influenced Cranmer in the compilation of the Book of Common Prayer.

Luther's successor at Wittenberg as leader of the Reformation there was Philip Melanchthon (1497-1560). Melanchthon had taught Greek at Tübingen, then at Wittenberg. Under Luther's influence he was transformed from a humanist to a theologian. He not only defended the teaching of Luther, but systematised it, producing the first real Protestant systematic theology – the *Loci Communes*. This had the effect of popularising the theology of the Reformation. Melanchthon believed that union with Rome was possible; in consequence, some of the Reformers viewed him with suspicion.

The Reformation – John Calvin
The greatest mind of the Protestant Reformation was undoubtedly John Calvin (1509-64). He was born in Noyon, France and was educated at Orleans and Paris. While studying in Paris he turned to Protestantism as a result of encountering the teachings of Luther. He began studying the Bible and in 1536, at the age of twenty-seven, he produced the first edition of the *Institutes of the Christian Religion*, a clear and definitive account of the teachings of the Reformation. That year, 1536, Guillaume Farel persuaded Calvin to move to Geneva, to consolidate the work of the Reformation there. There he met with opposition, and the following year had to leave and went to Strasbourg, where he met Martin Bucer. Calvin published his *Romans* commentary in 1539, the first of a prodigious output of biblical studies.

Calvin returned to Geneva in 1541 as leader of the Reformation. He wished to reform the city as well as the church, and bring the whole of civil life under church discipline. Many accepted his views, but others resented what they considered as an impudent outsider forcing his views on them. Calvin, however, wished to see the whole of Genevan life, in religion, education, politics and the arts brought under the influence of the Bible and the discipline of the church. He set up an Academy at Geneva, where students from all over Europe were taught biblical theology. This in turn became a missionary centre, sending preachers of the Reformation to all parts of Europe.

Calvin's great strengths were his ability to systematise the doctrines and organise the churches of the Reformation. The *Institutes* went through many editions in Calvin's lifetime and became the most influential dogmatics volume of the Protestant church. B.B. Warfield stated that 'the publication of the *Institutes* was not merely a literary incident, but an historical event, big with issues which have not lost their importance to the present day'.[98] 'It was he,' Warfield continues, "who gave the Evangelical movement a theology."[99] Yet 'Rabbi' Duncan was also right to say that '[t]here's no such thing as Calvinism. The teachings of Augustine, Remigius, Anselm and Luther, were just pieced together by one remarkable man, and the result baptised in his name'.[100]

Calvin worked and preached for over twenty years in Geneva until his death in 1564. He preached at least once every day, often delivering several lectures and sermons during the course of a week. He knew that the proclamation of the Scriptures was the only thing that the church needed. 'Sola Scriptura' was Calvin's watchword.

Calvin's successor in Geneva was Theodore Beza (1519-1605). He had been trained in law, and turned to Protestantism in 1548. He became Professor of Greek at the University of Lausanne. Calvin made him rector of the Genevan Academy, and he became a defender of the Reformed faith. He completed a translation of the Psalms, and was also one of the first biographers of Calvin. He was a fitting successor to Calvin and established Geneva as a centre of Protestantism.

It is worth noting that one of the reactions of the Roman Catholic Church to the growth of Protestantism was to call an important church council in Trent (northern Italy) in the mid-sixteenth century. The Council of Trent met in three sessions: 1545-7, 1551-2 and 1562-3. The third of these sessions was particularly important in defining Roman Catholic doctrine in terms of the beliefs of the medieval church, and modern Roman Catholicism appeals to Trent for its authority on many matters of the faith. The Jesuits were also a product of sixteenth-century Roman Catholicism. So too was the revival of the Inquisition as a deterrent to the Protestant movement.

The Reformation – England

In England the Reformation was carried out under Henry VIII, but it was not modelled on the continental reformation of Calvin and Luther. Henry was a sincere Roman Catholic, who was given the title 'Defender of the Faith' by the Pope because he wrote a work defending the sacramental position of the Roman Church. In consequence, the title has been carried by English monarchs ever since. He broke with the Papacy to secure a divorce from Catherine of Aragon. Part of Henry's influence was felt in the Anglican Church, which he came to dominate. However, in this connection, one of his wiser actions was to appoint Thomas Cranmer as Archbishop of Canterbury in 1532. As far as defending the faith was concerned, Cranmer proved more faithful than Henry, and in some of the king's later marital adventures Cranmer withstood the monarch. Amid the events of the period was a formal break of the Church of England with that of Rome, in which the English monarch, rather than the Pope, was declared head of the Church of England. This was not a thoroughgoing Reformation, but did mark a significant break with Papal domination.

Cranmer's influence was felt in the production of the first and second Books of Common Prayer, which were eventually adopted by the Anglican Communion. The Thirty-Nine Articles of the Church of England were also largely the work of his hand. Cranmer was eventually burnt at the stake; having recanted his faith he boldly denied his recantation as the flames took his life away from him.

Some of the other English Reformers of the period were:

Hugh Latimer (1485-1555) was educated at Cambridge, and appointed bishop of Worcester in 1535. He became a leading preacher in the English Church and was eventually martyred under Mary Tudor. It is reckoned that Queen Mary was responsible for the deaths of some 200 Protestant leaders during her five-year reign from 1553 to 1558, but this probably did more to strengthen the Protestant cause than to diminish it. Many fled to the continent during these killing times, where they came under the influence of the Reformation in Europe. Latimer popularised the Reformed doctrines of Cranmer.

Nicholas Ridley (1500-55) was also a graduate of Cambridge, who supported Cranmer's reformed doctrines and principles. He was chaplain to Cranmer and was appointed bishop of Rochester in 1547 and of London in 1550. He was a scholar, and gave robust intellectual backing to Cranmer in the publication of the Book of Common Prayer.

John Hooper (1495-1555) was educated at Oxford, and entered an Augustinian monastery. When he converted to Protestantism he fled the country and came under the influence of the European Reformation. He became a bishop and served at Gloucester and Worcester until he too was put to death by Mary.

Miles Coverdale (1488-1568) was also an Augustinian monk who converted to Protestantism. He is remembered for his role in the translation and publication of the Scriptures, assisting Tyndale in this work, and completing Tyndale's translation after his death. He was responsible for the publication of the Great Bible in 1539 (so-called because of its size, which meant its use was confined to churches) and the Geneva Bible (which appeared in 1560). He was bishop of Exeter and was exiled during Mary's reign.

Following the death of Mary, her half-sister Elizabeth as queen restored and established Protestantism in England; in spite of civil and political difficulties during her long reign (1558-1603), she had positive influences, establishing the liturgy and styling herself supreme governor, rather than head, of the Church of England.

These were aspects of Reformation within the Church. At the same time, however, a separatist movement was beginning in England. Although Elizabeth did much to reform the Church of England, many were unhappy with the episcopal government and the liturgical worship of the church, and wished to see the church reformed along continental lines. The result was that they separated to form their own churches. In this we see the beginnings of the Puritan movement. The Puritans wished to simplify the forms of service, the ceremonies of religious worship and even the style of church architecture. The leaders of the Puritan movement in Elizabethan England were Thomas Cartwright (1535-1603) and William Perkins (1558-1602). Some Puritans remained within the Anglican communion, but others set up independent congregations. With increasing pressure being brought to bear on them, some of the Puritans fled to Holland, while others at the beginning of the following century went to New England, where their influence became considerable. The universities of Harvard and Yale were centres of Puritan influence. The most famous Puritan emigration ship, the Mayflower, sailed in 1620. The seventeenth century was to be the golden era of Puritan theology and history.

The Reformation – Scotland

In Scotland the Reformation of the church had many long-lasting effects, not least in establishing Presbyterianism in Scotland. With many Scots travelling and studying on the continent, and with the

Scriptures readily available, it was inevitable that Reformation doctrine and ideas should percolate into Scottish church life. The legacy of the Celtic Church and the teachings of the Lollards (the Wycliffe preachers) made the Scottish church receptive to the Reformation.

The Reformation in Scotland was precipitated by the martyrdom of Patrick Hamilton (1504-28), the son of a noble house who had studied in Paris with a view to taking clerical orders. When he returned to Scotland and preached by invitation in St Andrews, it was clear that he had come under Reformation influences. He was charged with heresy and condemned to death. The martyrdom of George Wishart (1510-46), who had come under the influence of Latimer and the continental theologians, and who adopted Calvin's style of expository preaching in Scotland, was also a catalyst for the winds of change to blow throughout the church.

The man for the hour was John Knox (1514-72), a native of Haddington who entered the priesthood in 1536. By 1543 he was teaching in Haddington, and came under the influence of Reformation theology. In St Andrews in 1547 he felt a call to preach the gospel. During the next eighteen months Knox was a galley slave in France, and stayed for a while in England thereafter. He met with Calvin and other Reformed leaders on the continent and pastored an English congregation at Frankfurt for a short period in 1554 before returning to Scotland in 1559 and leading the Reformation there.

It is impossible in this short compass to do justice to the industry and effects of Knox's work in Scotland. The *Scots Confession* of 1560 was largely his work, which led to the Protestantising of the Scottish church. He wished to purify the church and society on biblical lines. He urged a simplistic style of worship and a biblically orientated style of government. That his remains should lie unmarked beneath an Edinburgh car park today is an affront to his memory and the legacy he left Scotland. He stood for Presbyterianism and an alliance with England against the Queen, who stood for Catholicism and an alliance with France. He saw the issues involved, and stood for a biblical form of government in Christ's church.

Knox's leadership role in the Scottish church was taken by Andrew Melville (1545-1622). A brilliant scholar, Melville would become principal of Glasgow University, then of St Andrews. Melville believed in the independence of the church from the state, the government of the church by general assembly, and the application of consistent, biblical church discipline. Melville encapsulated Knox's outlook in the claim he made before King James VI that there were two kings and two kingdoms in Scotland – the kingdom of Christ, where James was but a subject, and the civil kingdom in which he was a sovereign. Melville stoutly defended Reformed Presbyterianism, which was the mode of government in the Scottish church until James restored episcopacy.

The Seventeenth Century – Puritanism

Important dates

1611	Publication of the Authorised Version of the Bible
1620	Mayflower pilgrims sailed to America
1660	Restoration of King Charles II and the Anglican Church
1661	Beginnings of the Nonconformist movement
1682	Appearance of Bunyan's *Pilgrim's Progress*

The Reformation in Scotland was, as we have noted, a thorough-going one, which affected the whole of Scottish church life. In England, there was dissatisfaction with the extent of the change; although there were reforming movements and tendencies (most notably in the production of a thoroughly Reformed Book of Common Prayer, and the Thirty-Nine Articles), episcopacy and liturgy remained the hallmarks of the Anglican Church.

Within the Church of England itself, a new reform movement began, known as Puritanism. It is my belief that the rich legacy of Calvinistic and Reformed teaching was continued in the Puritan writings and tradition. Modern theology is not hospitable to this idea; some theologians have argued that the Puritans modified Calvinism by introducing legal and federal concepts into it which were alien to the thought of Calvin himself. This in turn, they say, led to Scottish church life being introspective and led to massive problems with assurance of salvation.[101]

This, however, is a false view both of Calvinism and of Puritanism. In both traditions the overwhelming desire was to return to a scriptural theology. Much of the modern view has been designed to accommodate the subjective and universalistic emphases of Karl Barth and to argue that Barthianism, and not Puritanism, is the more representative of Reformed theology.

On the continent of Europe, an important synod was held at Dordt in the Netherlands in 1618 to deal with some doctrinal difficulties which had arisen particularly among Dutch Calvinists. Jacobus Arminius (1560-1609) taught a form of conditional predestination, in which election followed grace, and was dependent on the free choice of man. His followers published their "Remonstrance" in 1610, which questioned some of the leading teachings of Calvinism. The Remonstrants grounded God's election in his foresight of faith, taught that Christ had died for the salvation of all men, said that grace could be resisted, and that perseverance was not necessarily guaranteed to all. The Synod of Dordt repudiated these positions and embraced a robust Calvinism which the Dutch church took as the confession and formulation of its faith.

When King James became king of England in 1603 he called a conference of bishops and clergy at which it was suggested that a new translation of the Bible be made. The translation was to be from the original manuscripts for use in all the churches in England. Forty-seven out of fifty-four nominated scholars took part in the work which began in 1607, with three groups working on the Old Testament, two on the New Testament and one on the Apocrypha. Two groups met at Oxford, two at Cambridge and two at Westminster. Strict rules were adhered to, which allowed for a revision of the translation(s) at every stage. The new version, the Authorised King James Version, was published in 1611, although it was not a new translation from the original but a revision of the Bishops' Bible of 1568 on the basis of the original, and it was never officially sanctioned by the church. The Geneva Bible remained more popular for the next half century, although gradually it was eclipsed by the Authorised Version, particularly following the restoration of Charles II in 1660. Perhaps Alister McGrath is correct to state of the Authorised Version that "the most significant factor in its final triumph appears to have been the fact that it was associated with the authority of the monarch at a time when such authority was viewed positively".[102] The Authorised Version is still rightly regarded by many as a faithful and accurate translation of the Scriptures, but we must guard against making use of it as a test of orthodoxy!

The Puritans

Who were the Puritans? J.I. Packer in his work *Among God's Giants* defines the Puritans this way:

> Puritanism I define as that movement in 16th and 17th century England which sought further reformation and renewal in the Church of England than the Elizabethan settlement allowed. 'Puritan' itself was an imprecise term of contemptuous abuse which between 1564 and 1642 ... was applied to at least five overlapping groups of people – first, clergy who scrupled about some Prayer Book ceremonies and phrasing; second, to advocates of the Presbyterian reform programme broached by Thomas Cartwright and the 1572 Admonition to the Parliament; thirdly, to clergy and laity, not necessarily nonconformists, who practised a serious Calvinistic piety; fourth, to 'rigid Calvinists' who applauded the Synod of Dordt and were called doctrinal Puritans by other Anglicans who did not; fifth, to MPs, JPs and other gentry who showed public respect for the things of God, the laws of England and the rights of subjects.[103]

It is important to note that the term 'Puritan' was a nickname – and not a very nice one. They were also known as 'Precisionists', because of the care they took over doctrinal formulation and the application of Bible truth in everyday life. They were concerned that the Settlement under Queen Elizabeth, which advocated Reformed doctrine but Roman Catholic practice in the church, did not go far enough. A half-reformed church was not the scriptural ideal. Oppression of the nonconformists went on over the turn of the century. When James I became king in 1603 the Puritans hoped that their situation might improve, but they came under the threat of the king. The publication of the notorious Book of Sports in 1618, which encouraged Sunday sports, was contrary to Puritan theology and they reacted against it.

Many Puritans found that they could not remain in England, and emigrated. The Mayflower sailed for Plymouth, Massachusetts, in 1620, leading to the beginnings of a strong Puritan influence in eastern America, which is still felt in the growth and influence of the universities of Harvard [founded 1636], Yale and Princeton (though many of these 'ivy league' universities have strayed far from their Puritan roots).

The accession of King Charles I in 1625 and the appointment of William Laud as Bishop of London in 1628 and Archbishop of Canterbury in 1633 led to further persecution against the Puritans. In 1640 the so-called 'Long Parliament' tried to set limits to the king's powers, and the partial success in this led to emigration to New England largely ceasing.

Following the Long Parliament, a special Assembly was convened at Westminster between 1643 and 1649 to consult on matters of church policy and doctrine. The Westminster Assembly produced radical and fundamental documents, such as the *Directory for Public Worship*, the *Westminster Confession of Faith*, and the *Larger* and *Shorter Catechisms*. These documents breathe the spirit both of the Reformation and the Puritan movements.

The Work of the Westminster Assembly (1643-47)

June 1643	Parliament authorises the convening of the Assembly
July 1643	Assembly meets in Westminster Abbey
September 1643	Assembly and Parliament sign the Solemn League and Covenant
January 1645	Parliament approves the Directory of Public Worship
December 1646	Confession of Faith presented to Parliament
August 1647	General Assembly of the Church of Scotland approves the Confession
October 1647	Assembly sends Larger Catechism to Parliament
November 1647	Assembly sends Shorter Catechism to Parliament
April 1648	Parliament receives final forms of Catechisms
February 1649	Last official session of the Assembly

In the civil war which followed these events, Oliver Cromwell (1599-1658), as head of a parliamentary army, and embodying the Puritan and reforming ideals, defeated the king's army. This not only ended the civil war, but also led, in 1646, to the abolition of episcopalianism in the Church of England. With the execution of Charles I in 1649, Cromwell took a leading role in government, and, as Lord Protector of England, tried to govern on Puritan and biblical lines.

With the accession of King Charles II in 1660, the monarchy was restored and so was episcopacy. In 1662 an Act of Uniformity was passed which required exclusive use of the Anglican Book of Common Prayer. This led to the resignation or ejection of many Puritan pastors. The liberty of the Puritans was not fully restored until the so-called 'Glorious Revolution' of 1688, when William of Orange and Queen Mary were proclaimed King and Queen of England.

Although distinct and separate events were taking place in Scotland at this time, these events were to have a profound effect and leave a precious legacy to the Scottish Church. The gospel we preach is the gospel of the New Testament, shaped by Calvin and informed by the biblical thinking of the Puritans.

Some notable English Puritans
The lives of the Puritans are shining examples of faithful Christian service. Some of the leading men of the Puritan movement were the following:

- Richard Sibbes (1577-1635) was born in Suffolk and educated at Cambridge; he preached at both Cambridge and London before returning to Cambridge. In many ways, he was the 'first' Puritan, and his thinking was influential; Richard Baxter came to faith by reading Sibbes' work, and Goodwin's theology was shaped by Sibbes' thought. Sibbes taught at Dublin and Cambridge, and became highly involved in controversies over church government, which itself divided the Puritans.

- Thomas Goodwin (1600-79) was ordained an Anglican vicar, but became an independent minister in 1634. Along with others he was harassed by Archbishop Laud and spent some time in Holland. He led the congregationalist party at Westminster and was one of Cromwell's advisers.

- John Milton (1608-74) was the great poet of the Puritan period. Laud's persecuting activities made him decide against entering the ministry. His *Paradise Lost* and *Paradise Regained*, as well as numerous other works, helped popularise the Puritan theology.

- Richard Baxter (1615-91) was a leading Anglican pastor and army chaplain. Packer has written of him that 'he exercised at Kidderminster, Worcestershire, the most fruitful Puritan pastorate anywhere recorded, converting almost the whole town'.[104] He declined the offer of a bishopric in 1660. He wrote constantly, and his massive output included gems like *The Reformed Pastor, The Saints' Everlasting Rest* and the *Call to the Unconverted*.

- John Owen (1616-83) was the great systematician of the Puritan tradition. He was the son of a Puritan vicar, and a native of Oxfordshire, graduating from Oxford. After a short pastoral ministry he returned to teach at Oxford and became Vice-Chancellor in 1652. He was also one of Cromwell's chaplains. Owen's stature as a theologian is undisputed.

- John Bunyan (1628-88) was the famous tinker-dreamer of Bedford, whose devotional and practical writings go to the very heart of experiential Christianity. He fought in the Parliamentary army and spent twelve years in prison, consistently refusing to accept freedom in exchange for his silence. Without formal education, he wrote over sixty works that married doctrine to life. *Grace Abounding to the Chief of Sinners* (1666) recounts his conversion, and *Pilgrim's Progress* (1682) tells the story of the Christian life.

- John Flavel (1630-91) was educated at Oxford and pastored at Dartmouth. Among his works are *Treatise on the Soul* and *The Methods of Grace*.

- Matthew Henry (1662-1714) was originally a law student before he entered the ministry. He was pastor of a church at Chester from 1687 to 1712. His great legacy was his commentary on the Bible (completed by others after his death) which is still highly used and commended.

There were many other faithful servants of Christ raised at this period as children of the Puritan movement. Although they all adhered to Calvinistic theology, they were not all agreed on other issues, particularly on the issue of church government. Of the above list, for example, Goodwin, Milton and Owen were congregationalists; Baxter was an Anglican; Bunyan was a Baptist; and Flavel and Henry were Presbyterians. While we are jealous for our distinctives, we must always acknowledge that there may be spiritual giants in other church traditions.

One book highly recommended for an overview of the Puritans is Leland Ryken's *Worldly Saints: The Puritans as they really were*. In it he lists what he calls 'Some Leading Traits of Puritanism':

- Puritanism was a religious movement
- Puritanism was characterised by a strong moral consciousness
- Puritanism was a reform movement
- Puritanism was a visionary movement
- Puritanism was a protest movement
- Puritanism was an international movement
- Puritanism was a lay movement
- Puritanism was a movement in which the Bible was central
- Puritanism was an educated movement
- Puritanism was a political and economic movement.[105]

We must also remember that as far as the larger picture is concerned, Puritanism was a failure. It did not fulfil its ultimate objective in effecting thorough reformation of the Church of England. Indeed, the Puritans lost almost all their battles. But those who love the truth of the gospel thank God for the Puritan tradition as the stream down which the doctrines of the Reformation were carried to us.

Two important legacies of the Puritan movement were the Westminster Confession of Faith and the colonisation of New England, where the Great Awakening was to reap such an abundant gospel harvest.

The Reformation Legacy in Scotland

From 1560 to 1600 the Reforming movement in Scotland continued under Knox and Melville. One of King James' aims was to strengthen his position north of the border, and he sought to suppress the holding of Assemblies on the part of the Church. In defiance of this, some ministers sought to hold an Assembly in Aberdeen in 1605, and were consequently imprisoned. Among them was John Welsh, Knox's son-in-law. As James sought to make the Scottish church conform to episcopal practice, Welsh and others stood for the sole Headship of Christ and the sole sovereignty of Christ in the Word.

In 1618 an important Assembly of the church was summoned by the King and met at Perth. The Five Articles of Perth were passed, which required the following:

- that the Lord's Supper should be received kneeling
- that the Lord's Supper may be administered in private
- that baptism might be in private
- that children should be confirmed
- that Christmas, Good Friday, Easter and Pentecost should be observed as holy days.

For those who stood in the stream of Calvinistic Puritanism, such requirements were an intolerable imposition. The Reformers of the period were anxious to have worship and liturgy governed by the Word of God, and as far as they were concerned, the requirements of Perth were an addition to the requirements of the Scripture, and therefore represented an intrusion into the domain of Jesus Christ, who alone governs his church through the Bible.

By the time of James' death in 1625, Melville had been banished, and the bishops had a stronghold in Scotland. King Charles and Archbishop Laud continued James' practice, and sought to implement episcopalianism in Scotland. In the High Kirk in Edinburgh on 23 July 1637 Dean Hannay officiated at a service during which he sought to implement Laud's liturgy. The story may be apocryphal, but it is too good to miss out: a devout, if over-zealous believer, Jenny Geddes, threw her stool at the Dean. A riot broke out in the High Kirk. Scotland had had enough, and a movement to re-establish the crown rights of Christ in Scotland began.

This movement led to the signing of the National Covenant in Edinburgh in 1638, which was the renewal of a pledge to honour Christ in church and national life. The National Covenant was largely the work of Alexander Henderson and Archibald Johnston. Modelled on the Reformed doctrine of the covenant of grace, the National Covenant was a bond between Scotland and the Head of Scotland's church. Signed in Greyfriars Kirk in Edinburgh, it became a popular catalyst for uniting disparate groups spread throughout Scotland, and ushered in the Covenanting period of Scottish church life. This was followed in 1643 by the signing of the Solemn League and Covenant, in the context of a desire for closer links between Scotland and England in the civil war. Robert Baillie said that the English were for a civil league, the Scots for a religious covenant. The terms of the Solemn League and Covenant provided for the maintaining of the Reformed faith in the Church of Scotland, and the Reformation of the church in England, with a view to uniformity in religion.

The Covenanters were supporters of these covenants. In the initial period afterwards, the Covenanting armies clashed with the armies of King Charles and many lost their lives under the banner of 'Christ's Crown and Covenant'. During Cromwell's Protectorate, the Scottish church enjoyed a measure of freedom in religion, but the restoration of Charles II in 1660 led to the Killing Times and to widespread persecution against the Covenanting cause. It was not until 1690, when Presbyterian government was restored in the Church, that the Covenanting ideals were met. The Westminster Confession was ratified as the Church's subordinate standard, patronage was abolished and the General Assembly resumed its place of authority and supremacy. When it met in 1690, it was the first such gathering for thirty-seven years.

A great deal happened in the seventeenth century, and this has been a short summary. Some of the leading figures of the time were the following:

- Alexander Henderson (1583-1646) played a leading role in the later Scottish Reformation. A native of Fife he was a graduate of St Andrews and a minister in Leuchars, Fife. He was not converted at the time of his ordination, and his appointment was against the wishes of the congregation. He became, however, a bright witness on the side of Christ. He denounced episcopacy and spoke out against the Five Articles. He was Moderator of the General Assembly in 1638, a recognition of the leading part he had played in the National Covenant and the Solemn League and Covenant. He was also leader of the Scottish Commissioners at Westminster. He died as minister of the High Kirk (St Giles, Edinburgh).

- Samuel Rutherford (1600-61) was one of Scotland's greatest theologians. He graduated from Edinburgh University in 1621. After studying divinity he became minister at Anwoth in 1627. Because of his nonconformity to the Articles of Perth he was exiled to Aberdeen. In 1638 he was appointed Professor of Divinity at St Andrews and wrote in defence of Presbyterianism. In 1643 he was one of the Scottish commissioners at Westminster, and was in London for four years, during which time he preached before Parliament. His writings cover not only theological, but also political subjects, and his *Lex Rex* (a philosophical treatment on the limits of a king's power) was one of the greatest political theories published, in which Rutherford argued that the power of the king is not absolute. His most popular work has been his *Letters*, written from exile in Aberdeen to persecuted members of his flock.

- George Gillespie (1613-1648) was the son of a minister of Kirkcaldy. After studying at St Andrews he was appointed a chaplain to the Earl of Cassilis and published a dispute against Popish ceremonies. After the signing of the National Covenant he became a minister in Fife and in 1642 became minister of Greyfriars Church in Edinburgh. He was also one of the Scottish Commissioners in Westminster (the youngest commissioner and an active participant). He was largely responsible for getting the Scottish General Assembly to approve the Confession of Faith and the Catechisms of Westminster.

- Richard Cameron (1648-80) was originally a schoolteacher; after hearing some of the persecuted field-teachers he allied himself with the covenanting cause. He alienated himself from some of the covenanters because of his extreme and outspoken views on government. On 22 June 1680 he and a group of his fellow-believers issued the Sanquhar Declaration, renouncing the authority of Charles II and declaring him a traitor. He was killed that year, and his head and hands put on display in Edinburgh. He was known as the Lion of the Covenant.

- James Renwick (1662-88) was the son of godly parents, and was educated at Edinburgh University. He graduated in the year that Donald Cargill was martyred (1681) and cast in his lot with the Covenanting cause. For seven years he preached faithfully and continued his studies in Holland. Some of his writings fuelled the fires of hatred against him, and he died in 1688, the last martyr of the Covenanting period, when he was only twenty-six-years old. He rejoiced to go to the scaffold, he said; this was a privilege not even the angels had. He told his fellow Covenanters: 'Keep your ground and the Lord will provide you teachers and ministers.'

Other events of the seventeenth century

The growth of the Baptist movement
Part of the nonconformist movement of the century was seen in the rise of the Baptist churches, generally dated from the Puritan John Smyth who went to Holland and baptised himself in 1608. There followed a growing movement which espoused the view that the Bible teaches that believers only – rather than infants – should be baptised. The first General Baptist Church commenced in London in 1612. Because of their insistence on having no connection with the state, they were often persecuted by King Charles.

The Thirty Years War
Just as the Puritan movement was caught up in the English Civil War, so Calvinists on the continent of Europe found themselves involved in an armed conflict. Between 1618 and 1648 the Calvinists and the

ics were involved in a long and bitter struggle. Germany was
vastated, but it did mark the end of religious wars in Europe.

The rise of the Quaker movement

In 1650 George Fox, a nonconformist preacher was jailed for six
months in Derby, England, for blasphemy. He had preached that Christ
had died to take away his sin. He told the judge to fear God; to which
the judge reponded by saying that Fox and his people were the ones
who should be afraid – they were the tremblers and the quakers. This
nickname stuck, and the Society of Friends, the Quaker Movement,
was born. It was really a revolt against dead, formal religon. At their
meetings anyone could speak. They were often in conflict, both with
the established church and with the other separatists. Their movement
spread to America, where one of the most famous Quakers, William
Penn, founded Pennsylvania.

The Enlightenment

The seventeenth century marked the beginning of the Age of Enlightenment. Philosophers such as René Descartes (1596-1650), Thomas
Hobbes (1588-1679) and John Locke (1632-1704), as well as scientists
like Isaac Newton (1642-1727), were to lay down principles of thought
which would revolutionise the worldview of this, and later, generations.
As part of the scientific 'progress' of Enlightenment thought, it became
a truism that the church had enslaved the thinking of people, with its
supernaturalism and its dogmas. It was necessary, so these thinkers
argued, to abandon such presuppositions and move knowledge forward
on a humanistic and rationalistic basis. Later thinkers in this tradition,
such as Immanuel Kant (1724-1804) would lay down the foundation
on which unbelieving biblical criticism would later build. Although the
Enlightenment produced a flowering of culture in the arts, its long-
term effect was to drive a wedge between faith and reason. For most
Enlightenment thinkers, religious faith was only a barrier to a true
understanding of the world, and of our place in it.

The Eighteenth Century – Revival

Important dates	
1703	Jonathan Edwards born
1714	George Whitefield born
1726	Beginnings of the Great Awakening
1738	'Conversion' experience of the Wesleys
1792	Baptist Missionary Society

There were two characteristics of the eighteenth century: first, that it was a period of revival, and second, that it was a period of evangelism and outreach. As the Word of God spread, and the doctrines of truth were disseminated following the Reformation and the Puritan movements, the Spirit of God came with power and revival blessing. As a result of this, there was much missionary activity in the eighteenth century, as the Pentecostal blessings had left the church going out with the gospel. Given the range of material available for the study of church expansion in the last three centuries, we will have to be even more selective than usual.

The eighteenth century was not free from controversy, nevertheless as a general guide we shall look at the two areas of revival and evangelism.

An Age of Revival
In his study of the church in the eighteenth century, A. Skevington Wood begins by saying that at the beginning of the century, 'Christianity had for the most part ceased to be a vital force. The spiritual life of the people had largely been smothered by the dense atmosphere of materialism.... There can be no serious uncertainty concerning the need for revival.'[106]

The history of the church has been punctuated by periods of revival, times of refreshing from the presence of the Lord. The fulness was poured out at Pentecost, but the same Spirit refreshes and visits the church to revive God's cause and maintain life in God's church. D.L. Moody probably went too far when he described Pentecost as a 'specimen day', but it was an error with a lot of truth in it. Scholars have pointed out that most of the revivals of the eighteenth century were within the Protestant church. That should hardly surprise us, because the truth of God's Word is at the heart of every revival, and the Reformation did nothing if it did not let the Word of God loose among people.

The revivals of the period took place mostly within the first half of the eighteenth century, from around 1711 to 1742. The following were among the most significant events during this period.

Wales[107]

God had witnesses for himself in Wales, some of whom, like their English counterparts in the seventeenth century, found themselves deprived of hearth and home through the cruel treatment meted out to nonconformist ministers. One of the first preachers of the Welsh revivals was Griffith Jones (1683-1762), who has been described as the morning star of the Methodist Revival. Jones was an Anglican vicar. Many clergymen of the Anglican church were more interested in worldly pursuits than spiritual ones, and this troubled Jones. His insistence on a spiritually devoted clergy got him into much trouble with church authorities. Jones made a great contribution to education in Wales.

He became a circuit preacher (in the manner still employed by Methodists), and met John Wesley and George Whitefield at one point. Denominationalism meant nothing to him, and he regarded all godly men with the same attitude of spirit, and did not hesitate to preach wherever he could find an audience.

Jones' influence in the Welsh revivals of the eighteenth century was felt, however, in the preaching of three of his famous successors.

The first of these was Howell Harris (1714-73), the son of a Welsh farmer. One of the gospel influences on his life was attending a communion service when the evangelical vicar, Pryce Davies, exhorted those who were not at the table, 'You plead your unfitness to come to the Holy Communion. Let me tell you, that if you are not fit to come to the Lord's Supper, you are not fit to come to church, you are not fit to live, you are not fit to die.' Refused ordination in the Anglican church four times, Harris remained a lay preacher throughout his life, both in North Wales and in the South. His home in Trevecca became a centre for mission work and the training of preachers. This was, in part, due to his association with the Countess of Huntingdon, who helped finance students to train and go out with the gospel. He was not an accomplished theologian, but he was a zealous evangelist, whose preaching was powerfully accompanied by the Holy Spirit. D. Martyn Lloyd-Jones says that Harris, following his conversion, had an experience of Holy Spirit blessing, and that this 'created within him a compassion for the lost'.[108] Harris has been described as 'the most successful preacher that ever ascended a platform or pulpit in Wales'.[109]

Another preacher who owed his work to Jones was Daniel Rowland (1713-90), who found himself an ordained Anglican minister although still unconverted. His ministry was to him only a means to get a livelihood. But a restlessness of spirit sent him to hear the independent preacher Philip Pugh, who drew large congregations to hear him and warned them of judgement to come. Rowland modelled himself on Pugh, and started thundering out in the same manner. To his surprise, the experiment worked, and his congregation grew. Hundreds were brought under conviction of sin, and Rowland was still unconverted. When they asked him 'What must we do to be saved?', he could not tell them. It was during the preaching of Griffith Jones that light dawned in Rowland's soul and thereafter he preached with great power. Howell Harris called Rowland a second Paul in his own pulpit. Many flocked to hear Rowland preach. Although his sermons were usually short, on one Sunday he preached for hours through the power of the Spirit.

A third spiritual son of Griffith Jones was Howell Davies, who was removed from his curacy in Llys-y-fran in spite of the obvious blessing attending his preaching. Many flocked to his tiny chapel, and often the sacrament had to be administered several times because of the crowd.

England

George Whitefield (1714-70) was a native of Gloucester, whose ministry took him all over the world. He was a student at Oxford when he was converted in 1735. The following year he was ordained and began preaching. An association with the Methodist movement began around this time, as did evidences of God's blessing accompanying Whitefield's work, while a young vicar of twenty-two.

Whitefield was to become the great evangelist of the evangelical awakening of the eighteenth century. He preached both throughout Britain and in the United States of America. Whitefield once said about faith that 'a true faith in Christ Jesus will not suffer us to be idle. No: it is an active, lively, restless principle; it fills the heart so that it cannot be easy till it is doing something for Jesus Christ.' It is reckoned that Whitefield preached over 18,000 sermons during his lifetime, consumed with a passion to make Christ known and to entreat men to come to him. He called himself 'one of God's runabouts', and preached as much out of church as in it.

The following extract from Whitefield's *Journals* proves this point:

> Aged 24 (1739) Saturday December 30th :
> Preached nine times this week, and expounded near eighteen times, with great power and enlargement. I am every moment employed from morning till midnight. There is no end of people coming and sending to me, and they seem more and more desirous, like new-born babes, to be fed with the sincere milk of the Word. What a great work has been wrought in the hearts of many within this twelvemonth! Now know I, that though thousands might come at first out of curiosity, yet God has prevented and quickened them by His free grace....Glory be to God...[110]

Whitefield was a burning and a shining light, and his work deserves to be remembered. He died in Massachusetts.[111]

The conversion of John (1703-91) and Charles (1707-88) Wesley was also of great significance during this period. Sons of an Anglican clergyman, their mother, Susanna, had a great influence on them. As students in Oxford, they started the 'Holy Club' there, and this bore its own fruit, not least in the conversion of Whitefield.

One of the Wesley brothers' first endeavours was to undertake a mission in Georgia in 1735. The following year, both of them, independently of each other, had powerful spiritual experiences. John Wesley says that at a meeting in London, when a passage from Luther's *Preface to Romans* was being read, his heart was 'strangely warmed', and this proved to be a turning point. The Wesleys were now deeply impressed with the need to bring the gospel urgently to the whole of Britain. Others preached in their parishes, but John and Charles preached wherever they found a hearing, and spread the Gospel through word and hymn. The beginnings of the Methodist movement are to be found in the itinerant preaching of the Wesley brothers. It is reckoned that John Wesley travelled over 250,000 miles in the service of the gospel of Christ, aggressively evangelistic for over fifty years.

Wesleyan doctrine was not always robustly Calvinistic. John could say in 1744, 'I love Calvin a little, Luther more.... Mr Whitefield more than either ... but I love truth more than all.' Perhaps, however, his difficulty was with the cold, uncaring, lifeless form of Christianity he found in established parishes and churches. 'I have one point in view,' he declared, 'to promote, so far as I am able, vital, practical religion, and by the grace of God to beget, preserve and increase the life of God in the soul of man.'[112]

America

In the previous century the Puritans had colonised many parts of New England. But within a century the fervour of the Mayflower pilgrims had all but gone, and the church in America was pretty much dead. Some of the late seventeenth-century Puritans such as Increase Mather could write books entitled *The Glory Departing from New England*. Part of the decline was a consequence of the so-called Half-Way Covenant, which was an arrangement whereby parents could baptise children in church without any major commitment to that church on their own part.

If ever a revival was needed, it was needed in Northampton, Massachussetts, when Jonathan Edwards (1703-58) became pastor there, following the faithful ministry of his grandfather, Solomon Stoddart. Edwards had a short ministry in New York and was a tutor at Yale University before coming to Northampton in 1727. In 1735 there was a remarkable spiritual awakening, which was repeated in the so-called Great Awakening of 1740. Edwards credits George Whitefield as the chief means by which the 1740 revival broke out, and in a letter to a Boston minister, highlights the following features: 'there was more seriousness and religious conversation, especially among young people; those things that were of ill tendency among them, were forborne; and it was a very frequent thing for persons to consult their minister upon the salvation of their souls.'[113]

Edwards wrote some useful works on the revival in New England: his *Narrative of Surprising Conversions* and his *Thoughts on the Revival* are extremely helpful works. In particular, he was aware that there were many false converts, and many over-zealous converts during the revival. He urged men not to judge the whole by a part, which is always an important principle. He was convinced that the revival was a genuine work of God even if parts of it were not held in check as they ought to have been.

Edwards regularly spent up to thirteen hours a day in his study. His mind was first-rate and he was a deep theologian. Yet under the preaching of Whitefield, whom he welcomed into his pulpit, he wept like a child. Both preacher and listener were in the midst of revival blessing and awakening.

Edwards was dismissed from Northampton in 1750, following a controversy over the Lord's Supper, and went as a missionary to Stockbridge where he preached to the Indians. In 1758 he became President of the College of New Jersey (now the University of Princeton), but died of smallpox two months later. His legacy is one of rich and full Calvinistic doctrine; his works deserve to be read.

Moravia

There was also revival in Europe during this period, particularly in Moravia (now part of Czechoslovakia). The church had been established by the eleventh century, but revival in 1715 led to the growth of the church in Europe. One central figure in the Moravian revival was Count Nicholas Zinzendorf (1700-60), a Lutheran nobleman who financed church building and planting. At a communion in 1727 there was a baptism of Holy Spirit blessing, which fuelled further evangelism and preaching. Although there were only six hundred people in Herrnhut, where Zinzendorf established his church, within twenty-five years some eighteen missionaries had been sent out with the gospel, and over two thousand in the course of the next century. The Moravian Church was a remarkable work of God. Among the beneficiaries of this revival were the Wesleys, whose contact with these Moravian preachers proved fruitful. Zinzendorf, for example, preached in England at John Wesley's request.

Scotland

Following the Union of the Parliaments in 1707, the liberties of the Scottish Church were safeguarded, although the use of the Prayer Book and the practice of Patronage were to remain as a feature of Scottish Church life for over a century. It is no exaggeration, however, to state that Christianity was ineffective throughout Scotland in this period, described by Thomas Chalmers as 'the Dark Age of the Scottish Church'. Part of the deadness was to be seen in the number of disruptions, secessions and schisms that punctuated Scottish church history during this period.

There were some outstanding evangelical preachers at the turn of the century. James Hog of Carnock (1658-1734) wrote many useful works and evangelical books. Thomas Halyburton (1674-1712) was Professor of Divinity at St Andrews and a great apologist for the faith. Hugh Martin describes Halyburton and William Cunningham as the two greatest theologians Scotland ever produced. One of Halyburton's theological concerns focused on the question of whether regeneration precedes justification (that is, whether the change of a man's nature precedes the change of a man's state).

Alexander Macrae, who wrote on *Revivals in the Highlands and Islands in the 19th Century,* devotes a chapter of his book to several revivals during the eighteenth century. There was a notable revival in Rosskeen, during the winter of 1742-3 under the preaching of Daniel Bethune. This revival seems to have affected many young people in the area. There were also movements of the Spirit of God in Sutherland, including a revival in Golspie in 1731, under the ministry of John Sutherland, and in Tongue in 1769, under Rev William Mackenzie. The most famous revival was that at Cambuslang in 1742, at which George Whitefield preached. Hundreds flocked to hear the gospel preached. It is estimated that at a high point in the revival, 40,000 people came to hear Whitefield preach in the open air.

Among the issues that affected the Scottish Church in the eighteenth century, three are worthy of mention.

Sandemanianism

John Glas was a minister near Dundee in the 1720s, who had difficulties over ministers signing the Solemn League and Covenant (because he believed that church and state should be separate) and also subscribing to the Westminster Confession of Faith (because he believed it should be enough for a man to say he accepts the Bible as his sole authority). His son-in-law, Robert Sandeman, was an aggressive controversialist, who wrote many books and championed Glas' views. Both of them were orthodox, staunch Calvinists, who wished to assert the authority of the Bible. Sandemanianism is the term used to describe the view of faith which they espoused, which emphasised that faith assents to the revealed doctrine of Scripture (a notional view of faith), without emphasising the subjective affections of the heart. It was enough, they believed, for a man to assent that the Bible was true.

Faith, of course, is not less than this. Those who have faith must believe that God exists and that he rewards those who seek him (Hebrews 11:6). For that to be the case, true faith must accept the premise that the Bible is the revealed word of God, and true in all it avers. But faith must be more than simply an intellectual assent to that proposition; there is an irony in a position which says that faith is merely accepting the truth of the Bible, when the Bible itself makes clear that faith also includes trust. Sandemanianism grew out of an objection to credal subscription and a wish to assert the sole supremacy of the Bible. In practice, this view objected to the whole notion of conviction of sin, and the preaching of the Law. It still flourishes today in the kind of preaching that plays down the role of repentance and conviction of sin. All that was necessary was to preach the Bible's evidence and men would believe. But it is not enough for preachers simply to present a case. Nor is it enough for hearers simply to assent to facts. Where there is faith there is earnestness in both preacher and hearer, because the issues of faith go deep into the hearts of men.

The Marrow Controversy

This was a celebrated controversy in the Church of Scotland between 1718 and 1723. The origin of the controversy is in a statement to which the Presbytery of Auchterarder required licentiates to subscribe. The statement, known as the Auchterarder Creed, made the following the confession of a licentiate: 'I believe that it is not sound and orthodox to teach that we must forsake sin in order to our coming to Christ, and instating us in covenant with God.' A young divinity student, William Craig, complained about this to the General Assembly, which in 1717 upheld Craig's case and accused the Presbytery of encouraging people to become spiritually slothful and thus weakening their obligation to gospel ordinances. What the Auchterarder Creed actually did was to safeguard the free and unconditional offer of the gospel – forsaking sin is not a condition that requires to be fulfilled before a man comes to Christ. It was sinners that Jesus came to save, not sinners who had forsaken their sin.

Following the Assembly's decision, Thomas Boston (1676-1732) recommended a book to a fellow minister. An introduction to Boston is necessary here.[114] Thomas Boston was a Church of Scotland pastor in Simprin in 1699 and Ettrick in 1707.[115] Boston had to deal with some of the extreme views of the Cameronian covenanters; in spite of the corruptions in the church, he argued that as Christ had worshipped in the Temple, so God's people ought to worship in church together.

'Rabbi' Duncan called Boston a 'commonplace genius'. He was an excellent linguist and a first-rate theologian. His *Human Nature in its Fourfold State* captures the biblical doctrine of man exactly. In 1747 Jonathan Edwards wrote a letter to Thomas Gillespie saying that the *Fourfold State* 'shows Mr Boston to have been a truly great divine'.[116] Principal John Macleod describes Boston as 'one of the brightest lights in the firmament of the Reformed Church in Scotland'.[117] In Boston there is a firm emphasis on covenant theology, with some personal distinctives. For example, the older Reformed School distinguished between the Covenant of Redemption (between Father and Son) and the Covenant of Grace (between God and His People in Christ as Covenant Mediator). Boston preferred to speak of one covenant of Grace, made with Christ as the Head, and his people chosen in Him.

While at Simprin, Boston came across *The Marrow of Modern Divinity*. This was a book written around 1645, and republished in 1718 with a preface by James Hog. This book fed Boston's soul and clarified his view of the free offer of the gospel. It was written in the form of a dialogue between Evangelista, a gospel minister, Nomista, a Legalist, Antinomista, an antinomian, and Neophytus, a young Christian. Part 1 deals with the Covenants and Part 2 with the law and its relation to the Gospel.

The appearance of the *Marrow* in the light of the Assembly decision meant that it became the focus of intense theological debate over the nature of the gospel. There was much written and verbal attack involving Boston, Hog and Principal James Hadow, who accused the marrow-men of universal salvation. The 1720 Assembly condemned the *Marrow*. The controversy drew the nation's attention to this book and came to a close in 1723. In essence the heart of the controversy revolved round the relationship between God's sovereignty and man's responsibility, and the way in which the gospel should be preached. While this controversy may be all but forgotten now, except perhaps to students of historical theology, there is no doubt that the great legacy of the Marrow controversy was that it bequeathed to the Scottish church a balanced view of the relationship between election and evangelism. It is possible (and, indeed, vital), to proclaim an unconditional and universal gospel while still holding to the biblical tenets of sovereign election.

The Erskines

Among the galaxy of godly men to grace Scotland were the Erskine brothers, Ralph (1685-1752) and Ebenezer (1680-1754). They seceded from the Church of Scotland in 1733, forming, along with others, the Associate Presbytery of the Secession Church. Their protest was against the Church's increasing toleration, in their view, of doctrinal error. For a while they flourished, and corresponded with Whitefield, whom they invited to Scotland to preach. But they fell out with Whitefield and ended up condemning him and the Cambuslang revival as being of the devil.

That, however, is a blot on an otherwise godly ministry exercised by these brothers at difficult times. 'God in Christ' was the theme of

Ebenezer Erskine's preaching. If the thesis of this book is true, that God has had a witness for himself in the darkest times of the church's history, then it is also true that in times of blessing and revival, the devil has never been far away, marring the witness of the Church and seeking to prevent the unity and harmony of the church from being realised.

Mission in the Eighteenth Century

The spiritual revivals of the eighteenth century fuelled the missionary impulse of the church. The church committed herself more and more to taking the good news to the world. Societies sprang up dedicated to this work. In 1698 the Society for the Propagation of Christian Knowledge was established and was instrumental in sending the Word of God throughout Britain and beyond (the Scottish SPCK was founded in 1709). The year 1701 saw the founding of the Society for the Propagation of the Gospel in Foreign Parts.

The same was true in Europe. German missionaries went to Holland and India. A missionary college was set up in Copenhagen in 1714. Count Zinzendorf, whose community of Moravian Christians was recognised as an episcopal church by an Act of Parliament in 1749, sent out Moravian missionaries to some ten countries.

Towards the end of the eighteenth century it was becoming clear that church structures of themselves could sometimes prevent mission, so Christians came together for the purpose of working towards that common goal. One of the most influential people in this connection was William Carey (1761-1834), the great Baptist missionary to India. In 1792 he published his *Enquiry into the Obligation of Christians to use Means for the Conversion of the Heathen*. That same year the Baptist Missionary Society was founded and the new century dawned with an aggressive attempt to bring the gospel into all the world.

The Nineteenth Century – Mission

Important dates

1804	Founding of the British and Foreign Bible Society
1817	Robert Moffatt began mission work in South Africa
1843	The Scottish Disruption: formation of the Free Church of Scotland
1859	Publication of Darwin's *Origin of Species*
1867	First Lambeth Conference
1870	First Vatican Council
1873	David Livingstone dies

The nineteenth century was a century of widespread change throughout society. Intellectually, these changes followed the Enlightenment movement of the past, and witnessed profound changes in scientific theory and study. Economically, the world was transformed by the Industrial Revolution, which had far-reaching consequences for society. This was accompanied by political changes, as socialism developed and led to the formation of modern political parties.

Following the evangelical revivals of the eighteenth century, missions and missionary work were to play an important role in the early years of the nineteenth century. It was to the church that the mandate was given by Christ to go into all the world and make disciples; but it was clear that individual churches – indeed, individual denominations – could not do this on their own. In order to enable the church to fulfil the Great Commission, one fruit of the evangelical revivals was the growth of missionary and Bible societies and organisations which saw the outposts of the world as a field, ripe for harvest, and sent labourers out into it.

India: William Carey

The Baptist Missionary Society was founded in 1792. The following year Carey sailed for India, and studied oriental languages for three years in Bengal. For the first quarter of the nineteenth century, Carey and two fellow Baptists organised the mission work in the vast Indian subcontinent. The New Testament was translated into Bengali, and Carey contributed a great deal to Indian education and culture. He founded the Agricultural Society of India in 1820, and encouraged Indians to witness as missionaries to their own fellow countrymen. He is perhaps remembered for his great motto: 'Expect great things from God; attempt great things for God.'

China: Hudson Taylor and William Chalmers Burns

James Hudson Taylor (1832-1905) was a Yorkshireman who was converted as a teenager and went to China in 1853 with the Chinese Evangelisation Society. He cut his connection with the Society and remained in China as an independent missionary. Because of ill-health he returned home in 1865, and founded the China Inland Mission that same year. This has been described as 'the first truly inter-denominational foreign mission'.[118] Hudson Taylor wished to evangelise every area of the Chinese Empire, and set standards for foreign mission work which were new at the time, but which set a pattern for modern mission work. For example, he insisted that missionaries should accept the dress codes of the native peoples of the lands they were working in. He also realised that it was important to keep Christians at home informed of what was happening on the foreign field, and made sure that information was widely available for this purpose. During a spell at home in England, many of his missionaries were killed in the Boxer Uprising of 1900. Hudson Taylor returned to China, and died there in 1905. The China Inland Mission continues its work under the name of the Overseas Missionary Fellowship.[119]

William Chalmers Burns (1815-68) was a brilliant divinity student of the Church of Scotland who left for China in 1847 (by which time he had joined the newly formed Free Church of Scotland). In Scotland, England and Canada his preaching had attracted large crowds. Then he was appointed a missionary to China by the English Presbyterian Church. In 1854 he was involved in a remarkable work of the Spirit of God in China. After a time in Scotland, he returned to China in 1864, where he died.[120]

Africa: David Livingstone and Mary Slessor

David Livingstone (1813-73) was born in Blantyre, Scotland. From 1841 to 1856 he served the London Missionary Society in South Africa, under Robert Moffat, whose daughter he married. Moffatt had arrived in South Africa in 1817, and had established mission work there. While building on this foundation, David Livingstone was also a pioneering missionary, exploring and evangelising territory hitherto unknown and uncharted. During his time in Africa he succeeded in walking further than any other traveller. He wanted to help the Africans; many of his troubles were with Europeans. Following his work there, the Scottish churches took up the challenge of African missions on a large scale.[121]

Mary Slessor (1848-1915) was born in Aberdeen, and after the family moved to Dundee in 1859, became a mill-weaver. She became a United Presbyterian Church missionary and arrived in Calabar in 1876. She became an important figure in Okoyong, where she later worked, and was a pioneer in changing some of the social customs of the area, including witchcraft trials and ritual killings. She became a well-known missionary in the African continent.

The Jews: Robert Murray McCheyne

The mission to the Jews was associated with a famous visit in 1839 by Robert Murray McCheyne, Alexander Keith and Andrew Bonar to Palestine. They published their *Narrative of a Mission of Enquiry to the Jews from the Church of Scotland* in 1839, which stimulated a great interest in Jewish mission work.

McCheyne (1813-43) was one of the century's great preachers. Part of his greatness was evidenced in the fact that when he arrived from Israel and discovered that a revival had broken out in his parish of Dundee through the preaching of William Chalmers Burns, he was full of praise and thankfulness to God. McCheyne always regarded himself as an evangelist, and was deeply concerned over the need for church extension and the evangelism of Scotland's towns and cities.

The Scottish Church in the Nineteenth Century

During the course of the century the Industrial Revolution brought thousands to live and work in the cities. The rise of the tenement city, with attendant problems of overcrowding and ill-health, brought a new challenge to the churches. The vast population was moving away from the countryside with its traditional industries and lifestyle. Although there were notable revivals during the course of the nineteenth century, it was also a time when ideas were in the boiling pot, and many new concepts arose, which were a challenge to the traditional teaching of the church.

The Disruption

In 1843 the crises which had arisen in the Scottish Church came to a head with the Disruption. This was a secession, or separation of 450 ministers from the Established Church of Scotland, on the grounds that the state was exceeding its lawful authority by interfering in the running of the Church. The evangelical leaders argued that the 'Disruption' in question was not a disrupting of the church, but of the relationship between Church and State. In particular, landlords were abusing their power by imposing ministers on congregations against the will of the people.

The most notable leader of the Evangelical movement at this time in Scottish history was Thomas Chalmers (1780-1847). A native of Anstruther, he became minister of Kilmany in Fife in 1803. In 1815 he became minister of the Tron, Glasgow, and in 1819 of St John's. In 1823 he was appointed Professor of Moral Philosophy at St Andrews, and in 1828 Professor of Divinity at Edinburgh. Following the Disruption, he was deeply involved in the construction of New College, Edinburgh, becoming its first Principal.

Chalmers had a first-rate mind, and wrote many treatises on philosophy. As a minister concerned for the relief of the poor in Scotland's cities, he was a social reformer. He believed that the parish was the natural and logical locus for the relief of the poor, and his work in Glasgow, though criticised both then and now, was a massive undertaking of organised help for those who needed it most.

But it was as leader of the evangelical cause that Chalmers excelled. Unconverted when he entered the ministry, he embraced the evangelical faith with a robustness that singled him out as a natural leader. The Disruption was preceded by the Ten Years Conflict, which raised the issue of the spiritual independence of the Church. In 1834 the Veto Act was passed in the General Assembly, under the influence of the Evangelical Party, to allow congregations to veto, or express their disapproval of, a minister who was forced on them against their consent. A famous test case was that of the Parish of Auchterarder, where the case reached the House of Lords. Another case which highlighted these issues was an induction in the Parish of Marnoch, which led to the suspension of seven ministers of the Presbytery of Strathbogie for proceeding with the induction in defiance of the General Assembly. The discipline was on the grounds that the seven had acknowledged the secular courts to be superior in spiritual matters to the judicatories of the Church.

The issue came to a head in 1843. Under the leadership of R.S. Candlish, Robert Buchanan and Hugh Miller, the Free Church of Scotland was formed on the basis of the principle of 'sphere sovereignty', that is, that a distinction would be maintained between church and state as twin spheres of government, both accountable to Christ, neither interfering with the other, but both supporting one another. The concern of the Church leaders was not to turn the Church into a democracy, but to ensure that the Headship of Christ would not be compromised by further state control. It has to be noted that the Disruption was an evangelical and spiritual phenomenon, although many have questioned the necessity, and particularly the long-term consequences of the fragmentation of the Scottish Church. Many evangelicals opted to remain within the Church of Scotland.

After the Disruption

The task the Free Church Assembly set itself was to produce a replica of the Establishment they had left. They accepted national responsibility, believing that the Establishment Principle was fundamental to national religion. By the time we come into the second half of the nineteenth century, the Free Church had made monumental gains, establishing churches throughout each parish and building schools and theological halls. The three main denominations in Scotland in the second half of the century were the Church of Scotland, with 460,464 members in 1875; the Free Church of Scotland with 256,554, and the United Presbyterian Church with 187,761.

The Churches and the Bible

Theological issues were at the heart of the Disruption and the Evangelical movement. Within thirty years of the Disruption the Free Church was embattled over the authority of Scripture. In her theological halls there was a new movement, which had imported the modern, critical views of Scripture from the continent, and which was attacking traditional Reformed and evangelical views. One of 'Rabbi' Duncan's most outstanding Hebrew scholars, Andrew Bruce Davidson (1831-1902) pioneered new views of prophecy and the religious development of the Old Testament. One of Davidson's pupils, William Robertson Smith (1846-94), became Professor of Old Testament at the Free Church College in Aberdeen, and he popularised the critical views of the Old Testament, which led to a theological controversy and battle for the remainder of the century.

It was not scholarship which weakened the Free Church's testimony in the nineteenth century. Some of the outstanding evangelicals were men of great intellect: Thomas Chalmers, William Cunningham (1805-61), Hugh Miller (1802-56) and others were giants in the area of academic scholarship. The Christian faith has nothing to fear from scholars. What weakened the Church's testimony was a scholarship which accepted a non-supernatural basis for the Bible. The rationalistic movement in Germany began with the principle that the Biblical documents are like any other source documents, reflecting different religious traditions and cultures, edited and put together like any other book.

This new outlook was replicated in England. The publication of *Essays and Reviews* in 1860 by some leading clergymen showed that fundamental and long-held attitudes to the Bible's inspiration and authority were being questioned and undermined. It was argued that the Bible should be read and understood like any other book, not elevated above any, with readers accepting that it might be mistaken in some of its assertions. These movements eroded a long-cherished confidence in the sufficiency and authority of Scripture.

The Scottish Churches and the Westminster Confession of Faith
Along with a changing relationship to the Bible went a changing
relationship to the Westminster Confession of Faith as the credal basis
of the Scottish Church. Before the Disruption there had been evidence
of a new theological outlook in preaching which lacked the precise
formulation of the Confession. One notable example of this was John
Macleod Campbell (1800-72), who was inducted to the parish of Rhu
in Dunbartonshire in 1825. He believed that the legalistic strain of the
Confession was a threat to individual assurance, and that a person
could only enjoy assurance of salvation on the basis that Christ had
died for everyone. Christ's death, he taught, had secured forgiveness
for all in this life, and faith believes this. Alongside this, he taught that
the traditional view of the atonement as penal substitution was flawed,
and that the atonement was grounded not in law but in the fatherhood
of God.

Macleod Campbell was deposed in 1831. He is today held high as
an example of a pioneer of the new gospel of universal atonement
and pardon which became prevalent in the later nineteenth century.
Following his deposition, he himself acknowledged that "our doctrine
and the Confession are incompatible". By 1866 the Free Church
Assembly was sounding more relaxed notes as far as credal
subscription was concerned, and the United Presbyterian Church had
already framed a Declaratory Act in 1879.

The dogmatic Calvinism of the Confession of Faith was also eroded
by the evangelistic campaigns of Dwight L. Moody and Ira D. Sankey
from 1873 onwards. The campaigns were for many a breath of fresh
air, as crowds flocked to hear the evangelists preach. There cannot
be any doubt that many did have a genuine conversion to Christ as a
result of these campaigns, but they proved a mixed blessing, and had
the effect of weakening commitment to Reformed and Calvinistic
doctrine. It was not now the rationalistic liberals who were rejecting
the predestination of the Confession, but those who claimed to stand
in the evangelical and missionary stream of the Disruption Church.
The result was the drawing up of a Declaratory Act in the Free Church
of Scotland in 1892, an event which precipitated the Free Presbyterian
secession the following year.[122]

One of the consequences of the new evangelicalism which emerged in the nineteenth century was the writing and publication of many evangelical hymns, warm with a devotional spirit of faith. The nineteenth century hymnwriters included Fanny Crosby and Frances Ridley Havergal. It is estimated that 'between 1800 and 1880, 220 hymn-books appeared within the Church of England alone'.[123]

The Churches and the Poor

During the nineteenth century there was also a change in the attitude of the Church to social problems. Although Chalmers had developed a system of poor relief to tackle social deprivation, the message of the Church was that one should accept the conditions, however hard, which Providence had ordained.

James Begg (1808-83) was one of the first to tackle this problem. As a minister in Newington, near Edinburgh, he was often decried because of his uncompromising stance on theological issues. But in the 1850s he was instrumental in setting up the Scottish Social Reform Association, which sought to tackle issues such as poor housing, reformation of land laws, and parliamentary justice. He was one of the first to direct the Scottish Church in the recovery of a genuine social concern.

Although in some cases social concern filled the gap caused by a downgrading of the Church's theological position, for others it grew out of an evangelical reading of the Bible. The Church went out to leaven society not because it had nothing to preach, but because the prophets of the Old Testament as well as Christ in the New, were interested in social issues, such as the poor, justice, and equality.

The same evangelical concern for the poor and underprivileged is what gave impetus to the campaign for the abolition of slavery by William Wilberforce (1759-1833). A Member of Parliament from 1780 onwards, he was often in contact with Thomas Chalmers; as historian David Bebbington notes, 'his conversion gave Wilberforce the dynamic to lead the campaign against the slave trade, which he had abominated since the age of fourteen.'[124] Also of note was the campaigning work of Lord Shaftesbury (1801-85), the great evangelical social reformer, who campaigned for improved factory working conditions. The evangelicals were to the fore in campaigning for reform of social conditions in the nineteenth century.

Developments elsewhere

The nineteenth century was one which elevated the human spirit. The publication in 1859 of Charles Darwin's *On the Origin of Species* laid the foundation for an evolutionary theory of man's origin that appeared, at best, difficult to reconcile with the Bible's account of the creation of all things by an Almighty God. Some theologians felt that evolution could be understood in the light of a particular reading of Genesis Chapter 1. But for many people the new science was an assault on long-held Christian beliefs. T.H. Huxley, 'the high priest of Darwinism,' popularised the theory of evolution and coined the term "agnosticism" to describe the position of those who could not accept the certainties of the Bible.

Philosophers such as Friedrich Schleiermacher (1768-1834), George Hegel (1770-1831) and Ludwig Feuerbach (1804-72) laid the foundation for a view of the world and religion which put man at the centre of life and learning. The knowledge of God (theology) became the study of man (anthropology). Karl Marx (1818-83) applied these attitudes to political and societal movements. For Marx, religion was simply a prop for the people, and the essence of society he believed was found in communal working. Communism was born out of a worldview that rejected traditional theism. Friedrick Nietzsche (1844-1900) regarded himself as a prophet of the God is Dead movement; he became the authority upon which Nazism was founded.

All of this had a powerful effect on theology and the Christian faith. Given the scientific doctrine of evolution and the philosophical questions raised about religion and traditional theism, new views of the Old Testament became current. Julius Wellhausen (1844-1918) taught that Hebrew religion was a development from primitive nomadic times to later formalised religion. D.F. Strauss (1808-74), Ernest Renan (1823-92) and F.C. Baur (1792-1860) taught that the historical Jesus could be understood in the light of religious trends in the first century, and that there was no need to believe the supernatural, 'mythical' elements of the New Testament. It could also, it was said, be demonstrated that there was a cleavage between the teachings of Jesus and those of Paul.

This destructive, critical attitude to the Bible was a feature of nineteenth-century biblical scholarship. In Scotland, God raised up men like William Cunningham and Hugh Miller, who engaged with current trends and sought to answer them. In America, one of the most powerful forums for the defence and articulation of the Christian faith was to be found at Princeton Seminary, Philadelphia.[125] Archibald Alexander (1772-1851) was founder of Princeton Theological Seminary and first Professor of Theology there. Charles Hodge (1797-1878) became Professor at Princeton in 1822. He has been described as 'the premier Reformed theologian of America's nineteenth century'.[126] Although hospitable to some aspects of Darwinism, Hodge was a force to be reckoned with in the defence of biblical truth amid the ferment of ideas breaking ground in the nineteenth century. So too was his son, successor and biographer, Archibald Alexander Hodge (1823-86). Their works owed much to Scottish philosophy and theology, and in turn were much appreciated by Scottish Calvinists.

Other conservative, Calvinistic scholars in the American tradition included the following.

- James Henley Thornwell (1812-62) laboured as pastor and teacher in South Carolina. He had "a passion for orthodoxy and a sense of duty to truth, and he sought to defend traditional institutions and standards against liberal and ungodly assaults".[127] Of Thornwell's appointment to be Professor of Didactic and Polemic Theology at Columbia Theological Seminary, Douglas Kelly says that he "filled this post with brilliant distinction; he continued to be an outstanding preacher, teacher, writer, theologian, educator, ecclesiastical statesman, venerated public figure and devoted husband and father".[128]

- Robert Lewis Dabney (1820-98) was a native of Virginia who taught theology at Union Theological Seminary in Virginia. He was also a shrewd commentator on the civil war of the 1860s. Dabney has been described as a "thoroughgoing Calvinist" who nonetheless was not afraid to strike an independent note in discussing some theological questions.[129]

- Benjamin Morgan Palmer (1818-1902), who was also a pastor and teacher in South Carolina. Two of his main concerns were that the church should maintain a high view of Scripture and a high view of the doctrine of election.

Given the work being done in other places for the emancipation of slaves, it may strike us as strange that some of the theologians of the Southern States should defend slavery, or, as it was known, the institution of 'domestic servitude' in their writings. Douglas Kelly is right, however, to remind us, in discussing Thornwell, for example, that he was 'strongly influenced by the views of his culture, with the natural result that of course he had what later generations would see as glaring blind spots'.[130]

* Geerhardus Vos (1862-1949) was a Dutch emigrant to the United States, who became Professor of Biblical Theology at Princeton in 1893. He has been described as 'the father of a Reformed biblical theology',[131] that is, of a reading of Scripture which emphasises both the unity and continuity of biblical revelation.

The Great Awakening of the eighteenth century led to a debate in America in the nineteenth over the nature of revival. One of the men at the centre of this was Charles Grandison Finney (1792-1875). He professed to be a Calvinist, but his Calvinism was highly modified. His preaching was successful, partly as a result of new trends and the new methods he employed, such as the role of women and the use of inquiry rooms. He is rightly termed a revivalist, since he believed and taught that it was possible to make a revival happen, with the right use of methods and means. Finney's strength was his insistence on our responsibility and the need for our obedience; his weakness was in his dethroning of God's sovereign work in sending forth revival blessing.

In 1870 the First Vatican Council was held. It bequeathed to the Church the dogma of papal infallibility. This unbiblical doctrine was the natural outcome of the exaggerated claims of the bishop of Rome for himself over many centuries. The doctrine of infallibility while speaking *ex cathedra* was not new, but it was now officially taught and promulgated.

One of the great phenomena of the nineteenth century was the ministry of Charles Haddon Spurgeon (1834-92). Son of an independent minister, Spurgeon became a Baptist village preacher while still in his teens, and exercised a powerful ministry at New Park Street Chapel and then at the specially erected Metropolitan Tabernacle in London. He was thoroughly Reformed in doctrine, but did not believe in infant baptism. He left the Baptist Movement in 1887 during the so-called downgrade controversy, in which the authority of the Bible was being eroded. The publication of his sermons and commentaries fed the souls of thousands, and do still. His ministry was rich in doctrine and application, and the church was blessed indeed when God called Spurgeon to be a preacher of the gospel.

The nineteenth century was a full century. It was a time of new things, new ideas, of change and development in society and in philosophy. In some ways this had a disastrous effect on theology and Bible studies. Yet God maintained his cause, as in all eras of the Christian Church.

The Twentieth Century – Maturity

Important dates

1910	Edinburgh Missionary Conference
1919	Publication of Karl Barth's *Commentary on Romans*
1948	World Council of Churches set up
1949	Beginnings of Billy Graham's evangelistic work
1962-5	Second Vatican Council

The events in the Scottish Church at the end of the nineteenth century culminated in the Union of 1900 between the Free Church of Scotland and the United Presbyterian Church of Scotland to form the United Free Church of Scotland. The moves to introduce a Declaratory Act into the Free Church of Scotland in 1892 had led to the Free Presbyterian secession the following year. It is a moot point whether the remnant who remained faithful to Free Church principles in 1900 ought to have left in 1893. The minority argued that since the Formula signed by ordinands had not been changed, irrespective of the Declaratory Act having been passed, office-bearers were still bound to an unqualified and unmodified commitment to the Confession of Faith. They also believed that the Declaratory Act was passed with union as the aim and purpose in view, and that it was better to wait until the action had run its course before precipitating action by secession. One of the first actions of the continuing Free Church of Scotland after 1900 was the repeal of the Declaratory Act, and an offer of union with the Free Presbyterian Church. That offer was not taken up, and to the present time the two denominations have existed independently of one another.

The United Free Church was a large and influential denomination in the first quarter of the century. A House of Lords ruling in 1904, however, declared that the minority who had not entered the union to be the rightful owners of the property of the Free Church of Scotland.

The majority, therefore, found themselves homeless and churchless (although this was rectified through Parliamentary involvement later). It meant that the United Free Church found herself open to approaches from the Church of Scotland, offering her practical help in the first instance, and then offering co-operation and eventual union. These approaches were driven by a wide ecumenical impulse. Union negotiations began in 1909 and culminated twenty years later with the union of the two bodies to form the present Church of Scotland, which may be dated from 1929.

Theological Developments of the Twentieth Century

If the nineteenth century pioneered some new ideas in biblical and theological studies, these were developed into the twentieth. Three theologians in particular were to lay the foundation for a new approach to Scripture and a new attitude to the Gospel.

The first of these was Karl Barth (1886-1968). Barth was a Swiss theologian who had studied under some of the leading continental teachers of Germany. While pastoring at Safenwil in Switzerland from 1911 to 1921 he wrote an important commentary on Romans. In it, Barth took issue with the extreme liberalism of his day and sought to bring God into the centre of theological enquiry and Biblical study. He developed this in his voluminous series of *Church Dogmatics*. He recovered the supernatural emphasis of the Bible, but opened the door to an unashamed universalism.[132] His teaching found a sympathetic ear with Thomas F. Torrance, who was Professor of Christian Dogmatics at New College Edinburgh from 1952 to 1979. Torrance did much to domesticate Barth and Barthianism within mainstream Scottish theology.

A second influential theologian this century was Rudolf Bultmann (1884-1976), a distinguished New Testament scholar who studied and later taught in Germany. Bultmann's starting-point was that modern science had made the Bible's supernaturalism unintelligible to modern man. If the gospel was to be preached at all, the Bible had to be *demythologised*, and written in terms of a world-view that conformed to modern scientific enquiry and insight. Another way of describing Bultmann's approach is *existential*, in that it made the existence and experience of man normative for theology.

A third theologian of significance was Emil Brunner (1889-1966), another Swiss pastor-theologian who also stood in the stream of Barth and Bultmann. Brunner's emphasis was on revelation as a person-to-person meeting or encounter. Christian theism is only valid when it is authenticated in personal experience. There is no objective revelation or truth, no objective atonement because there is no objective sin/guilt doctrine. Similarly the Bible is not to be identified with the Word of God; it is only such when it becomes the Word of God to me. Brunner was a universalist, whose influence served to establish man as the centre of theology.[133]

Although Barth and Brunner are hailed as exponents of the Reformed tradition, their teaching and theology has served to weaken the commitment of the Reformed churches to the authority of Scripture, and to the nature of the atonement. Some of the leading exponents of classic Reformed orthodoxy in these areas were the following:

- Benjamin Breckinridge Warfield (1851-1921) was a student of Charles Hodge who travelled and studied in Europe before ministering in Baltimore and then teaching in Pennsylvania. He succeeded A.A. Hodge as Professor of Theology at Princeton. As well-known for the lavish attention he poured on his disabled wife, Anne, as for his defence of Reformed doctrine, Warfield did the church a great service by his insistence on an inspired, authoritative and infallible Bible. His studies in the thought of Calvin and Augustine renewed interest in the study of these great leaders of the faith. His great legacy was 'his exposure and refutation of liberalism's naturalistic worldview and reinterpretation of traditional Christian teaching'.[134] He was concerned that liberalism weakened Biblical truth by elevating man and by misinterpreting the work of Christ. To quote from Warfield himself:

The confession of a supernatural God, who may and does act in a supernatural mode, and who acting in a supernatural mode has wrought out for us a supernatural redemption, interpreted in a supernatural revelation, and applied by the supernatural operations of His Spirit – this confession constitutes the core of the Christian profession. Only he who holds this faith whole and entire has a full right to the Christian name: only he can hope to conserve the fullness of Christian truth. Let us see to it that under whatever pressure and amid whatever difficulties, we make it heartily and frankly our confession, and think and live alike in its strength and by its light.[135]

- J. Gresham Machen (1881-1937) was the son of a prominent Baltimore lawyer who studied classics and became a classical scholar of repute. At Princeton Theological Seminary he studied philosophy, and in 1905 studied New Testament in Europe, returning as teacher to Princeton where he eventually became Professor of New Testament. His great theological contribution was in defence of the New Testament against liberal and modernistic attitudes. His book on *The Origin of Paul's Religion* in 1921 defended the view that Paul's religion was not different to that of Christ. *The Virgin Birth of Christ* (1930) was a defence of the supernatural mode by which the incarnation took place. His work in 1923, *Christianity and Liberalism*, put forward the view that Christian and liberal worldviews are fundamentally opposed. These views led to confrontation within a changing Seminary and church and, consequently, to the founding of Westminster Theological Seminary in 1929, and the formation of the Orthodox Presbyterian Church in 1936.

- Cornelius Van Til (1895-1987) was a native of the Netherlands whose family emigrated to America in 1905. He studied at Calvin College, before taking up theological studies at Princeton. He ministered for a short while in Michigan, before teaching for a year at Princeton until he became a founding member of the Westminster Faculty in 1929. Van Til combined the American Reformed stream of Warfield and Geerhardus Vos with the Dutch stream of Abraham Kuyper and Herman Bavinck. He laid much emphasis on the Creator-creature distinction of the Bible, and insisted on pre-supposing the self-attesting God in dialogue with non-believers. He countered the views of Barth in a series of important publications such as *Christianity and Barthianism* and *The Defense of the Faith*.

* John Murray (1898-1975) was a native of Sutherlandshire, Scotland, brought up in a Free Presbyterian tradition. His intention to study for the ministry in that denomination led to his pursuing theological studies at Princeton. The tide of his life turned from the pastoral ministry to theological teaching. Having fulfilled a commitment to teach for one year at Princeton, he joined the faculty of Westminster, where he taught Systematic Theology until his retirement in 1966. Murray sought to apply the fundamental insights of biblical theology to Systematics, and did some important work in various areas of dogmatics, such as the doctrine of imputation and the doctrine of redemption. His *Redemption Accomplished and Applied* is one of the finest treatments of the atonement available, although Murray's ability to compress – to use one word packed with meaning – makes his writing difficult for many. Nonetheless, in spite of questioning some traditional formulations, he was an important influence on evangelical theology.

In many ways, these men in the old Princeton tradition laid down the foundation for modern evangelical theology and Reformed thought, on which many faithful expositors and teachers have continued to build. Although liberal thought continues to dominate many divinity faculties and schools, there are still many colleges all over the world committed to a robust intellectual defence of evangelical truth.

The Twentieth Century: the wider picture

The Ecumenical Movement

In June 1910 an important missionary conference was held in Edinburgh, convened at the Assembly Hall of the United Free Church of Scotland. The Conference was designed to address the needs and issues of modern missionary work, such as the message of Christian missions to non-Christian faiths, the preparation of missionaries, and the relation of missions to governments. However, the significance of the conference was much greater than that. Out of the discussions there were formed the Universal Christian Conference on Life and Work in 1925, and the World Conference on Faith and Order in 1927, two organisations that joined to form the World Council of Churches in 1948. The WCC was established at Amsterdam on the basis of the confession: 'The World Council of Churches is a fellowship of Churches which accept our Lord Jesus Christ as God and Saviour.' In spite of later alterations to this basic affirmation, other doctrinal issues continue to raise their heads, such as the nature and administration of the sacraments, and the role of ministry (including that of women).

The WCC was the beginning of the modern ecumenical movement. The word 'ecumenical' (like the word 'catholic') is a good word – it was used to describe the councils of the early centuries, which represented the views of the whole church throughout the world ('ecumenical' = 'the inhabited world'). Although only Protestants attended the Edinburgh Missionary Conference, the WCC today embraces many diverse churches and, as an organisation, its unity is more fundamental than truth or biblical authority. This is reflected in Scotland today in movements such as ACTS (Action of Churches together in Scotland). Movements such as the British Evangelical Council and the Evangelical Alliance seek to foster a biblical ecumenism that has its basis in an evangelical commitment, and allows different churches which are committed to the supremacy of Christ and the authority of the Scriptures to work together on a variety of issues.

Scholarship

While many of the theological departments in the mainstream universities have continued to build on the liberal scholarship of the nineteenth century, there has been a remarkable growth and development in evangelical scholarship all over the world. This has largely been concentrated in independent or church-affiliated schools and seminaries. In some traditions – not least in some trajectories of Scottish Presbyterianism – the emergence of liberal thinking *within* church-sponsored institutions led to a suspicion of scholarship. It became equated with unbelieving approaches to the Bible which played down the need for the supernatural work of the Holy Spirit. Yet where evangelical scholarship has paid attention to the human features of the Bible, using specialised skills to deal with issues of language, history, context and transmission of the text, a robust appreciation of Christian doctrine has emerged. Moises Silva is right when he states that 'not just our exegetical labors, but every aspect of our existence … must be integrated to our Christian identity, and that means prayer, a spirit of obedience, and the commitment to subsume everything under the great goal of sanctifying God's name'.[136] Many scholars have acquired exegetical and theological skills, often, ironically, by detailed research in university faculties, which they have in turn devoted to the cause of evangelical scholarship. In my view, at the present time, the future for such scholarship is very positive and bright.[137]

One of the most significant points for twentieth-century theological scholarship was the discovery of the Dead Sea Scrolls in the Qumran caves in Palestine. The first of these finds was in 1947. Fragments of biblical manuscripts, older than any in existence at that time, were among the finds. The collection of manuscripts also yielded a fascinating insight into life in the community which had hidden the scrolls in the first place, a community which was probably contemporary with John the Baptist and the early New Testament age. This discovery revolutionised some areas of biblical studies, since it opened a window on life in the time of Christ, as well as yielding some important historical documents.

Theological reflection is never static. The twentieth century witnessed two world wars (1914-19 and 1939-45), both of which raised issues which were of relevance to the church. During the First World War, many church leaders in Scotland were of the view that this 'solemn purification by fire'[138] might lead to a sense of the need for nations to turn to God. The war was regarded as a kind of chastisement for a nation's having forgotten God. But when the war did not produce a revival of interest in religion, many were disillusioned. The second war raised difficult theological questions, not least on account of the Holocaust, and the suffering of the Jewish people. Why should God allow such a thing to happen? And were the Christian churches to blame for this anti-Semitic behaviour? A major influence on theological reflection over the war years was Dietrich Bonhoeffer (1906-45). Executed in the closing months of the war, his legacy has been to relate theology to questions of politics and universal brotherhood.

In addition to traditional theological disciplines – biblical theology, systematic theology and historical theology – the twentieth century also witnessed the development of liberation theology. With the publication, in 1971, of *The Theology of Liberation*, written by a priest in Peru, the church began to relate her doctrine to the situation of the poor in Marxist-dominated countries. Liberation theology emphasises the place of the poor in the teaching of Jesus Christ, and offers a critique of any political system which seeks to dominate the underprivileged in society.

But even within the evangelical tradition, theology has shown that it is capable of development. In the 1980s, several evangelical scholars produced books suggesting that traditional evangelical views of God as the sovereign Lord who foreordains all things were not true to the biblical picture, and were unhelpful for Christian living. This led to the beginnings of a debate on 'open theism', the view that biblical statements such as God changing his mind and being ignorant of the future should be taken at face value, and that our concept of God should include the realisation that he collaborates with us in the fulfilling of his purpose.[139] This development is set to dominate theological reflection within evangelicalism well into the twenty-first century.

The American Evangelistic Movement

One of the phenomena of the twentieth century has been the ministry of Billy Graham on the international stage. The Moody and Sankey campaigns of the nineteenth century were, as we saw, a mixed blessing for Scotland, in that while they alerted the churches to the need for more concentrated evangelistic effort, they imported much into Scottish church life that was inimical to the robust Calvinism of an older day.

In some ways these problems continued to dominate evangelism into the twentieth century. The most famous evangelist of the twentieth century has been Billy Graham (born 1918). His visits to London and Glasgow in the 1950s resulted in a new wave of American mass evangelism. The more cynical would say that Billy Graham's success was a result of the post-war disillusionment which affected the nation in the middle of the century. Whatever our view, it is clear that many people were affected by the message of the gospel. In some ways the Billy Graham crusades stand as an indictment against the church for her lack of evangelistic zeal and endeavour. Billy Graham's preaching, though Arminian, has made Christ real and has proclaimed a full and free gospel. Graham has been followed by evangelists like Luis Palau, and more recently by his own son Franklin. The whole American mass evangelism movement has spawned a new day of televangelism and of multi-million dollar investment in the 'Gospel industry', not all of which has been helpful.

The Pentecostal and Charismatic Movements

One of the main growth areas of the twentieth century was the rise of Pentecostal and Charismatic churches. Deriving their names from the Day of Pentecost, when the outpouring of the Spirit led to tongue-speaking and miraculous signs, and from the Greek word *charis*, meaning 'grace' or a 'gift', Pentecostals believe in the ongoing nature of these gifts and signs. Although varieties of Pentecostalism differ, they have often been seen as a vital alternative to dead formalism in mainline churches. Pentecostalism spread first in the USA and in Latin America, but the modern Charismatic movement has spread all over the world. Christopher Catherwood suggests that 'Pentecostalism is the fastest growing wing of Protestant Christianity'.[140]

The charismatic movement has grown out of a deep sense of dissatisfaction with traditional mainstream church life. Often the concepts of ordained ministry and of structured organisation have been regarded as hindrances to the work of the Holy Spirit. But this is to belie the whole history and phenomenon of revival, which has been *within* the church, and often unaccompanied by external signs. If we truly believe in the sufficiency of Scripture, we will not require signs, which Christ told us an unfaithful and adulterous generation would seek after.

At the same time, the Charismatic movement has forced the mainstream denominations out of their traditionalism and lethargy, to ask pertinent questions about the ongoing and abiding witness and power of the Spirit in the Christian life and in the Christian church. We have been forced to ask whether, in fact, our pre-concerns with forms and with traditions have quenched the Spirit. Are we open to the Spirit? Are we baptised with the Spirit? These are legitimate theological questions which the church needs to keep asking herself.

But there has been another off-shoot of the charismatic movement.

Many mainstream denominations have been forced to ask hard questions about forms and styles of worship and liturgy as a result of the growth of the movement. Several Christian writers refer to 'worship wars' within the churches! The modern charismatic movement has brought diverse musical styles, dancing, drama and an increasing freedom into worship, which does not sit easily alongside many forms of worship elsewhere. Even within traditional denominations, debates over worship styles often dominate discussion.

Roman Catholicism

Although for centuries, as we saw, the light of God's revelation and the truth of the gospel was kept alive through the monasteries and the missionaries of the Roman Catholic Church, the Protestant Reformation raised a banner of truth against the unbiblical doctrines and practices of Rome. The last century has not seen the Roman Church loosen its grip on its traditional formulas or dogmas, and it has managed to retain the loyalty of its adherents much more than the mainstream Protestant denominations. There have been seven popes during the twentieth century, and the Roman Church has consolidated its position on many traditional dogmas. In 1950 the Bodily Assumption of Mary was decreed as an article of faith, and through increasing dialogue between the Anglican Church and the Roman Church, close links between the two have developed apace. The Second Vatican Council which met at Rome from 1962 to 1965 was a bold step on the part of Pope John XXIII to summon bishops from all over the world to discuss the need for reform within the Roman Church. The emergent Church was fully committed to all the traditional dogmas of Rome, but with a new shape, fitted to serve a new generation.

Towards the end of the twentieth century, the emergence of Evangelicals and Catholics Together (ECT) in America has raised new questions and issues regarding the scriptural authority for evangelistic and doctrinal co-operation between Protestants and Roman Catholics. It is doubtful, in spite of the fact that the movement has attracted some leading evangelicals, whether the benefits of such dialogue will outweigh the drawbacks.

Bible Translation and Mission Work

Since the Second World War, the Word of God has continued to be published in many languages and many forms. In particular, the work of the Wycliffe Bible Translators, represented in over forty countries, has ensured that the interdenominational effort to send out the Word of God in all the languages of the world has been co-ordinated well. It is reckoned that the Bible is now available in some 1,600 languages, although there are still many peoples throughout the world who have no access to a version of the Bible in their own language.

The publication of modern versions continues to fuel debates within churches. The New American Standard Bible (1962) and the New King James Version (1982) have sought to preserve the faithfulness of the King James Version to the original texts, while offering the translation in a modern idiom. Probably the most popular version in use by modern evangelicals is the New International Version (1978, revised 1984). Recently, evangelical Bible translation teams have produced the New Living Translation (Tyndale, 1996) and the English Standard Version (Collins, 2002). Part of the stated purpose of the NLT was to 'overcome some of the barriers of history, culture and language that have kept people from reading and understanding God's word',[141] while the ESV is hailed as an 'essentially literal translation that seeks as far as possible to capture the precise wording of the original text and the personal style of each Bible writer'.[142] These publications show the continued burden within the evangelical world to engage in translation and distribution of God's word. All translations, of course, have their merits and demerits – there are 'version wars' just as there are 'worship wars'! The current state of the Bible version debate is over the use of gender-inclusive language – for example, if the original says 'man', is it legitimate to translate this as 'person'? It may seem a small point, but it has actually caused major divisions and debates between academic evangelical scholars.[143]

The growth of Bible translations has gone hand-in-hand with the growth of missionary activity. Interdenominational missionary work has developed through missionary societies, with new technology allowing communication on an unprecedented scale. Christianity has continued to develop within the third-world countries, which has added its own complexion to theology.

The Story of the English Bible

Date	Translation	Individuals involved
1360-64	Wycliffe Bible	John Wycliffe and friends
1525-30	Tyndale Bible	William Tyndale
1560	Geneva Bible	English Puritans in Geneva
1604-11	Authorised Version	English scholars commissioned by King James I
1881-85	Revised Version	English scholars
1901	American Standard Version	American scholars
1946	Revised Standard Version	International Committee
1958	The New Testament in Modern English	J. B. Phillips
1961	New English Bible	British scholars, notably C. H. Dodd; New Testament in 1961, Old Testament in 1970.
1963	New American Standard Version	American evangelical scholars; New Testament in 1963, Old Testament in 1970.
1966	Jerusalem Bible	Roman Catholic translation
1966	Good News Bible	Robert Bratcher; New Testament in 1966, Old Testament in 1976.
1973	New International Version	Committee of evangelical scholars; New Testament in 1973, Old Testament in 1978.
1982	New King James Version	Committee of evangelical scholars.
1996	New Living Translation	Evangelical scholars from all over the world
2001	English Standard Version	Evangelical scholars from all over the world

Movements of the Spirit of God

Much of what I have written in these chapters has focused on the church in the West, and in Great Britain in particular. But the story of church growth in the East in recent times is also important and, in many cases, quite thrilling. Patrick Johnstone observes that the growth of Christianity in the non-Western world is now outstripping its influence in the West: 'In 1960, about 58% of professing Christians lived in the West (Europe, North America and the Pacific). By 1990 this had fallen to 38% and by 2000 it will probably be 31%.'[144] While this ought to give us pause in evaluating the direction in which the Western Church is going, it ought to thrill us and motivate us to further prayer and consecration as we see the harvest fields of the gospel continuing to yield fruit for Christ.

In South Korea for example, there has been remarkable blessing and revival since the first Protestant church was established there in 1884. Some of the world's largest congregations are to be found in the capital, Seoul, which is almost fifty per cent Christian. American evangelist Billy Graham held his largest evangelistic campaign in South Korea in 1973. In the closing years of the twentieth century there was a remarkable upsurge in theological training, Bible and book distribution and widespread penetration of the country with the Gospel.

In China, where Marxism moulded the politics and atheism brainwashed generations of children, the Christian church grew at an unparalleled rate in the last quarter of the twentieth century. We have already noted some of the missionaries who had a vision for China, and saw great potential there. In spite of many years of persecution against Christians, revivals have led to a widespread acceptance of the Christian faith. Although it is now difficult to send missionaries to China, the house-church movement has resulted in many thousands coming to faith in Christ. Chinese Christian literature has been in great demand.

In Asian countries, such as Kazakhstan, which was deeply influenced by Communism over many years, there was a great need for gospel witness, which has recently begun to be met. Mission agencies such as the Slavic Gospel Association report much encouragement in the planting of new congregations and churches in such areas.

There are indigenous groups too, like the gypsy peoples of Europe, who have responded to the gospel in recent times. In France and Spain, for example, the Christian gypsies are reckoned to be the largest group of evangelical Christians in these countries.

There have also been remarkable movements of the Spirit of God in South America. Brazil, which has the largest Catholic population in the world, now has the third largest evangelical population in the world, and missionaries are involved in training native Brazilians to take leadership roles within the church. Similarly Argentina's cities have witnessed spectacular revival and fruitful evangelism. Latin America seems ripe for gospel work and harvest.

This is truly a thrilling picture. In lands which were once closed to missionaries and evangelists, the collapse of communism has allowed entry with the gospel. In parts of Eastern Europe, for example, there is a renewed thirst for the gospel and an increased interest in Reformed Theology. Yet it is a picture that disguises a sobering reality, for it has been estimated that more Christians have been martyred for their faith in the twentieth century than in all the other centuries combined. If we truly believe that Jesus is Lord of his church, as he is Lord of history, then we need to pray that he will continue to strengthen his cause and his people for continued faithful witness in his name.

The Challenge for the Church

What are we to do with this great legacy of twenty centuries of church history and Christian proclamation and theology? Whatever our personal traditions, if we are the modern-day disciples of Jesus Christ, then two things are vital.

First, we must appreciate our past. The study of church history may appear to be a barren intellectual and academic exercise. To research the past is no less than an academic exercise, of course, and we ought to encourage the discipline of ecclesiastical history. I lament the fact that at the time of writing there are few church historians to be found in the Scottish universities. There is much to be learned from searching out our roots.

But the reading of church history is not the preserve of academics. It is a vital component of our Christian service. Even the New Testament urges us to remember those who told us about the gospel (Hebrews 13:7). To read Christian biography and church history is to be reminded of what God has done in the past in fulfilling his purpose to build his church in the world. The truths of the gospel are timeless, but each generation of believers has had to witness to, and contend for, the faith at specific points in the history of the world. What others did in their day, we are called to do in ours. We are not called to fossilise the past, or pay it undue homage. Nor are we to retreat into some golden age of Christian history. We are called to appreciate our heritage, in order that we may build on it, and so serve our own generation by the will of God. The Christian faith, as Mark Noll reminds us, has an "irreducibly historical character".[145]

Second, we must use our past to shape our present and our future. All that has taken place in the last twenty centuries provides us with a foundation upon which we may live and serve the Lord now. The story is, after all, unending. It began in eternity, with God's purposes of sovereign, free election, and will end in eternity, with the consummation of all things in Jesus Christ. While this world lasts, the purposes of God's grace in Christ have a very historical dimension to them. And in the present day, we are called to learn from the church of the past, from its successes and failures, from its progress and regress, from its advancement and declension, in order that we may the better continue to obey the Great Commission of Matthew 28:19-20, and make disciples for Christ until the end of the age. That means at least four things.

Maintaining and Defending the Truth

The church remains the pillar and ground of the truth. She is mandated to maintain the proclamation of the Word of God in all its glorious fullness, and defend and assert that truth before an unbelieving world. We need scholars to systematise our theology; to set it forth in a logical and Biblical manner, and to defend it against the mindset of an unbelieving world. We need to be aware of the full orbit of biblical revelation, the implications of biblical statements, the context of the biblical world and the central elements of the biblical world-view. Otherwise the Bible cannot be our rule for glorifying and enjoying God.

Given that it is our rule, we need to continue with the task of Bible translation and distribution. The King James Version is not the last word in this great task. The twenty-first century has its own distinctives, not least in its rejection of absolute truth and its acceptance of all outlooks. We are mandated to formulate and disseminate the truth of God's Word in such a world, and, within its rich cultural, linguistic, philosophical and religious diversity, to witness to the Lordship of Christ over all of creation, and his uniqueness as the only way to God.

Continuing to proclaim the gospel, using means traditional and new

It is through the foolishness of *preaching* that God has purposed to bring sinners into his kingdom (1 Corinthians 1:21). There are things which preaching can achieve which no other medium of communication is able to achieve. It is the continued duty of the Church, as in the past, to maintain the preaching of the gospel, in a way that handles the exegesis of the Bible expertly and proclaims it articulately and with relevance.

But the proclamation of the gospel is not to be confined to the pulpit. Just as the first-century believers spread the gospel through the highways of the Roman Empire, we are to spread the good news through the superhighway of the computer internet age, whose potential for evangelism is staggering. By computer link, as well as by means of other technologies, the church is able to access parts of the world with an immediacy which previous generations would not have imagined possible. Already there are many Christian resources on the Internet (not least for the study of church history!), and in a cyberspace world we have an opening to follow the example of past missionaries and to let the world know about Christ.

Raising voice about social issues

There is always the danger of the church becoming only an institution for public reform, rather than a dynamic body boldly preaching Jesus. Yet a church which does not raise a voice about society is not standing in the stream of the prophets or apostles; she is not following on from the work of the Reformation leaders or the Disruption fathers. There are numerous social issues that are affecting our society: unemployment, drugs, drink, abortion, euthanasia, homosexuality, the use and abuse of the Lord's Day. The Bible has something to say on each of these issues, and there is a need to search the Bible for the answers our society needs to hear.

It was Jesus himself who counselled his followers to be in the world but not of it (see John 15:19), and there is always a balance to be struck between our engagement with our culture and our counter-cultural mission. The Lord is our example here, as in all else. He was radically involved with the poor and disenfranchised, the marginalised and the oppressed. He was engaged with the culture of his day, from the carpenter's shed to the synagogue, from the wedding at Cana to the supper in the leper's home. But his contribution to his culture was that he brought the Word of God to bear on the outlook and philosophy of his day. Similarly we are called to be his followers in our own age, and not in any other, and our greatest contribution to our culture will be in our distinctiveness from it, as a people who have been set free by the truth.

Building up the fellowship of the body of Christ

Above all, believers need to strive together and stand together for the faith of the gospel. There is a need to learn from the past that we may see further into the future and put our trust in the one who is building his Church. We have a duty to do good unto all men, particularly those who are of the household of faith. We are called to repent of our fragmentation, our unholy divisions, and to seek the good of Zion, with the prayer that God might bless the church and revive his work in our day. There is, after all, one church, one faith and one baptism. All who call God 'Father' are brothers and sisters to us.

May God grant a continued increase to the work of his church into the next century and beyond!

FOR FURTHER READING

Although many historical studies are available for specific periods, I have confined this list to books which give a general survey of church history and historical theology, and on which I have drawn heavily in my study. Books dealing with different periods in the history of the Church may be found in the footnotes. I hope that they will give further help and be of use. Not all are written from an evangelical point of view. They are listed in alphabetical order of authors.

Douglas Andsell, *The People of the Great Faith: The Highland Church 1690-1900*, Acair, 1998 (an extremely helpful volume for anyone interested in the church of the Highlands and Islands of Scotland).

David W. Bebbington, *Evangelicalism in Modern Britain: A history from the 1730s to the 1980s*, Routledge, 1989 (a clear and very useful summary of 250 years of evangelicalism in Britain).

Gerald Bray, *Biblical Interpretation, Past and Present*, Apollos, 1996 (an excellent evangelical overview of the work done in biblical scholarship throughout the history of the Christian Church).

Peter Brown, *The Rise of Western Christendom*, Blackwell, 1997 (a detailed survey of the first thousand years of church history, which also contains useful comparative chronologies).

Nigel M. De S. Cameron (editor), *Dictionary of Scottish Church History and Theology*, T and T Clark, 1993 (indispensable for study of the Scottish Church, containing useful helps for further reading).

Christopher Catherwood, *Crash Course on Church History*, Hodder and Stoughton, 1998 (part of a 'Crash Course' series of readable books from Hodder. Well-presented and easy to read).

Christopher Catherwood, *Five Leading Reformers*, Christian Focus Publications (studies of the lives of Martin Luther, Ulrich Zwingli, John Calvin, Thomas Cranmer and John Knox).

Vivian Green, *A New History of Christianity*, Sutton Publishing, 1996 (a full survey of two thousand years of church history; contains a useful and comprehensive chronology).

Darryl G. Hart (editor), *Dictionary of the Presbyterian and Reformed Tradition in America*, IVP, 1999 (useful summary of the American scene, containing a wide variety of articles).

Patrick Johnstone, *Operation World*, OM Publishing (an indispensable treasure-trove of statistics and analyses of countries, showing how the gospel is impacting nations across the globe).

Donald K. McKim (editor), *Historical Handbook of Major Biblical Interpreters*, IVP, 1998 (a collection of many articles on various Bible scholars from patristic times to the present day).

Nicholas R. Needham, *2000 Years of Christ's Power, Part One: The Age of the Early Church Fathers*, Grace Publications Trust, 1998 (the first of an extremely promising series covering the twenty centuries since the birth of Christ to the present day).

Mark Noll, *Turning Points: Decisive Moments in the History of Christianity*, IVP, 1997 (Noll selects some dozen or so points which he regards as crucial in the history of the church, and examines their significance).

A.M. Renwick and A.M. Harman, *The Story of the Church*, IVP, 1985 (another general survey of church history, written from an evangelical viewpoint. Dr Renwick was Professor of Church History at the Free Church College, and his work has been brought up to date by his son-in-law, Prof. Allan Harman).

Leland Ryken, *The Puritans as they really were*, Zondervan, 1990 (an excellent introduction to the Puritans, studying their attitudes to various subjects, theological and practical).

Williston Walker, *A History of the Christian Church*, T & T Clark, 1970 (a detailed and comprehensive summary of church history).

Michael Walsh (ed), *Dictionary of Christian Biography*, Continuum, 2001 (a new and comprehensive dictionary giving biographical outlines of over 6000 people of varying degrees of significance in the Christian Church).

There are numerous other general and specialised studies of church history, too many to list here. But I hope that this will stimulate further interest in the fascinating story of the church of Jesus Christ from Galilee two thousand years ago to the present day.

Endnotes

Introduction
[1] A.A. Hodge, *Commentary on the Confession of Faith*, London, 1870, p. 64.
[2] Robert L. Dabney, *Discussions*, Volume 2, Banner of Truth, 1982, p. 23.
[3] Dabney, *Discussions,* p. 23.
[4] John Murray, 'Common Grace', *Collected Writings*, Volume 2, Banner of Truth, 1977, p. 113; cf. Robert L. Reymond, *A New Systematic Theology of the Christian Faith*, Thomas Nelson, 1988, pp. 399-403.
[5] William Cunningham, *Historical Theology*, Volume 1, Banner of Truth, 1969, p. 36.
[6] cf. A.C. Cheyne on 'Ecclesiastical History' in *Disruption to Diversity: Edinburgh Divinity 1846-1996*, T&T Clark, 1996, p. 110, who endorses the view that ecclesiastical history is 'a secular discipline with a theological perspective'.
[7] D. Martyn Lloyd-Jones, *The Puritans – their Origins and Successors*, Banner of Truth, 1987, p. 216.
[8] Cunningham, *Historical Theology*, p. 8.

The First Century – Beginnings
[9] J. Gresham Machen, *The New Testament: An Introduction to its Literature and History*, Banner of Truth, 1976, p. 33.
[10] For further reading on this theme, see Donald Macleod, 'Jesus and Scripture,' in P. Helm and C.R. Trueman (eds.), *The Trustworthiness of God*, Eerdmans, 2002, pp. 69-95.
[11] Geza Vermes, for example, in his seminal work *Jesus the Jew*, London, 1994, begins with the (general) reliability of the gospel writers, and contrasts his 'guarded optimism concerning a possible recovery of the genuine features of Jesus' with the 'historical agnosticism' of Rudolf Bultmann (p. 235).
[12] For the issues involved in this, see Craig L. Blomberg, *Jesus and the Gospels*, Apollos, 1997.
[13] B.B. Warfield, *The Lord of Glory*, London, 1907, pp. 275-76.
[14] A.M. Renwick and A.M. Harman, *The Story of the Church*, IVP, 1985, p. 23.

The Second Century – Expansion

[15] Cunningham, *Historical Theology*, especially pp. 35-42; Mark Noll, *Turning Points*, IVP, 1997, especially the introduction pp. 11-20.

[16] See Reymond, *Systematic Theology*, p. 65.

[17] D.A. Hagner, in *Dictionary of the Later New Testament and its Developments*, IVP, 1997, p. 87.

[18] Nick Needham, *2000 Years of Christ's Power*, Grace Publications Trust, 1998, p. 59.

[19] See further the discussion in Needham, *2000 Years*, Chapter 3.

[20] Needham, *2000 Years*, p. 68.

[21] 'Rabbi' Duncan is reported as saying in the *Colloquia Peripatetica* (edited by William Knight, Edinburgh, 1871) p. 37: 'It is a monstrous thing that that horrible word "heresy" is now used on all occasions so freely and applied so recklessly to all error. All error is not heresy.... Heresy is a work of the flesh and no man can be charged with it, even on a fundamental, till, after faithful admonishment, he persists in it, knowing that he does so.'

[22] Williston Walker, *A History of the Christian Church*, T&T Clark, 1970, p. 55.

[23] Louis Berkhof, *The History of Christian Doctrines*, Banner of Truth, pp. 56-57.

The Third Century – Consolidation

[24] As cited in Needham, *2000 Years*, pp. 100-1. On the phrase 'He descended into Hell,' see below.

[25] For a discussion of this issue, see Wayne Grudem's article, 'He did not descend into Hell: A Plea for following Scripture instead of the Apostle's Creed,' in *Journal of the Evangelical Theological Society* 34:1 (March 1991), pp. 103-13.

[26] Walker, *History*, p. 72.

[27] Walker, *History*, p. 74.

[28] Renwick, *Story of the Church*, p. 47.

[29] Walker, *History*, p. 96.

The Fourth Century – Controversy

[30] Walker, *History*, p. 102.

[31] Vivian Green, *A New History of Christianity*, Sutton Publishing, 1996, p. 24.

[32] Needham, *2000 Years*, p. 203. Some historians put the figure at

around 220 bishops.

[33] This extended version of the Nicene Creed appears in Gerald Bray, *Creeds, Councils and Christ,* Christian Focus Publications, 1997, pp. 206-7, and is the text adopted by the International Consultation on English Texts, subsequently adopted into the Church of England Service Book. The phrase 'and the Son' is bracketed to show that it was inserted later. The original Nicene Creed ended with 'we believe in the Holy Spirit'. See p. 48.

[34] Translation from (ed.) J. Stevenson, *Creeds, Councils and Controversies*, London, 1966, p. 148.

[35] Bray, *Creeds,* p. 129.

[36] Green, *New History,* p. 59.

[37] Duncan, *Colloquia Peripatetica,* pp. 38-39.

[38] David L. Smith, 'Divorce and Remarriage from the early church to John Wesley,' *Trinity Journal*, 11:2 (Fall 1990), p. 133.

[39] B.B. Warfield, *Calvin and Augustine*, Presbyterian and Reformed, 1980, p. 322.

[40] Donald Meek says that 'Many troubles await us in our search for his identity'! (*The Quest for Celtic Christianity*, Handsel Press, 2000, p. 128).

The Fifth Century – Definition

[41] Berkhof, *History of Doctrines*, p. 137.

[42] As cited in Walker, *History*, p. 139.

[43] Bray, *Creeds*, pp. 150-71.

[44] See G. Grogan, *The Christ of the Bible and the Church's Faith*, Christian Focus Publications, 1998, p. 233. Dr Grogan asserts that the creeds 'were intended to exclude heresy, not to give full positive expositions of the truth'.

[45] Renwick, *Story of Church,* p. 59.

[46] Walker, *History*, p. 141.

[47] See Meek, *Quest,* for a thorough discussion of the issues involved in studying the subject of Celtic Christianity. See pp. 131-33 for an introduction to Patrick, including a discussion of the difficulty of sources.

The Sixth Century – Fallout

[48] Bray, *Creeds*, p. 163.

[49] See Needham, *2000 Years,* pp. 324-30 for a discussion of the

various parties which vied for attention and supremacy in the aftermath of Chalcedon.

[50] Walker, *History*, p. 127.

[51] John Mackay, *The Church in the Highlands*, London, 1914, pp. 9-10.

[52] Mackay, *Highlands*, p. 18.

The Seventh Century – Challenge

[53] B.W. Sherratt and D.J. Hawkin, *Gods and Men: A Survey of World Religions*, London, 1972, p. 86.

[54] W.H. McNeill, *A World History*, Oxford, 1979, p. 221.

[55] Charles Hodge, *Systematic Theology*, abridged edition, Baker, 1988, p. 358. Emphasis mine.

[56] See Donald Macleod, *The Person of Christ*, IVP, 1998, pp. 178-80.

[57] Wayne Grudem, *Systematic Theology*, IVP, 1994, p. 561.

[58] See Meek, *Celtic Christianity*, pp. 169-70.

[59] Renwick, *Story of Church,* p. 68.

[60] Green, *New History*, p. 54.

[61] P. Brown, *The Rise of Western Christendom: triumph and adversity AD 200-1000*, Oxford, 1996, p. 165.

[62] There are always exceptions to such generalisations, of course. But it was true of the West that during these centuries it had 'sunk back towards barbarism, retaining only tattered shreds of classical learning, literature and art', McNeill, *World History,* p. 238.

[63] Gerald Bray, *Biblical Interpretation Past and Present*, IVP, 1996, p. 148.

The Eighth Century – Christendom

[64] H. Daniel-Rops, *The Church in the Dark Ages*, tr. A. Buther, London, 1960. This is the title of Chapter 5.

[65] Walker, *History,* p. 184.

[66] Walker, *History,* p. 185.

[67] Daniel-Rops, *Dark Ages,* pp. 401, 408.

[68] Quoted in Richard Fletcher *The Conversion of Europe*, p.182.

The Ninth Century – Darkness

[69] Daniel-Rops, *Dark Ages*, p. 405.

[70] Daniel-Rops, *Dark Ages*, p. 411.

[71] Bray, *Biblical Interpretation,* p. 148.
[72] Quoted in Walker, *History,* p. 192.
[73] Daniel-Rops, *Dark Ages,* p. 458.
[74] Green, *New History*, p. 70.

The Tenth Century – Instability
[75] Bray, *Biblical Interpretation,* p. 148.
[76] Walker, *History*, p. 200.
[77] Green, *New History*, p. 64.
[78] M. Macaulay, *Aspects of the Religious History of Lewis*, nd, pp. 6-7.

The Eleventh Century – Crusade
[79] Walker, *History,* p. 201.
[80] Walker, *History,* p. 202.
[81] M. Walsh (ed.), *Dictionary of Christian Biography*, Continuum, 2001, p. 549.
[82] Quoted in Green, *New History,* p. 89.
[83] Renwick, *Story of the Church,* p. 92.
[84] Green, *New History,* p. 89.
[85] Walker, *History,* p. 220.
[86] R.A. Finlayson, *The Story of Theology*, p. 37.

The Twelfth Century – Learning
[87] A.N.S. Lane, 'Peter Abelard,' in *New Dictionary of Theology*, IVP, 1988, p. 1.

The Thirteenth Century – Domination
[88] Renwick, *Story of the Church*, p. 93.
[89] Described in the *Dictionary of Christian Biography* as 'a great theological synthesis of theology and a comprehensive statement of his mature thought on all the Christian mysteries; it proceeds through objections and authoritative replies in each article to a concise summary of his views on the matter under discussion, after which the various objections are answered' (p. 1103).

The Fourteenth Century – Schism
[90] Green, *New History,* p. 87.
[91] Green, *New History*, p. 87.

[92] Walker, *History*, p. 275.

[93] Walker, *History*, p. 277.

The Fifteenth Century – Dawn

[94] Philip McNair, 'Seeds of Renewal,' in *The History of Christianity: A Lion Handbook*, 1977, p. 355.

[95] Walker, *History*, p. 283.

[96] P. McNair, p. 347

The Sixteenth Century – Reform

[97] J.I. Packer, 'The faith of the Protestants' in *Lion History*, p. 374. Packer does not mean by this phrase that we can interpret the Bible any way we like; he means rather that we are not reliant on any ecclesiastical authority to interpret it for us. The Reformation succeeded precisely because the Bible, interpreted within its own parameters, was given to the people.

[98] Warfield, *Calvin and Augustine*, p. 7.

[99] Warfield, *Calvin and Augustine*, p. 22.

[100] Duncan, *Colloquia Peripatetica*, p. 9.

The Seventeenth Century – Puritanism

[101] See, for example, T.F. Torrance, *Scottish Theology from John Knox to John McLeod Campbell*, T&T Clark, 1996, esp. chapter 4, 'The Westminster Tradition.' Cf. also the review article on this volume by Donald Macleod in *Evangelical Quarterly* 72:1 (2000), pp. 57-72.

[102] A. McGrath, *In the Beginning: the Story of the King James Bible*, Hodder and Stoughton, 2001, p. 289. This is an excellent telling of the story of the AV's publication and eventual triumph: see especially Chapter 12 for a discussion of the ascendancy of the AV over the Geneva Bible.

[103] J.I. Packer, *Among God's Giants: The Puritan Vision of the Christian Life*, Kingsway, 1991, p. 41.

[104] *New Dictionary of Theology*, p. 82.

[105] L. Ryken, *Worldly Saints: the Puritans as they really were*, Zondervan, 1990, pp. 10-14.

The Eighteenth Century – Revival

[106] A. Skevington Wood, *The Inextinguishable Blaze: Spiritual*

Revewal and Advance in the Eighteenth Century, Paternoster Press, 1967, pp. 7, 24.

[107] For an overview of God's work in Wales, see William Williams, *Welsh Calvinistic Methodism*, Bryntirion Press, 1988.

[108] Lloyd-Jones, *The Puritans,* p. 292.

[109] Wood, *Inextinguishable Blaze*, p. 51.

[110] *George Whitefield's Journals*, Banner of Truth Edition, 1960, p. 195.

[111] John H. Armstrong's book *Five Great Evangelists*, Christian Focus, has useful chapters on Howell Harris and George Whitefield. See also John Pollock, *Whitefield the Evangelist*, Kingsway, 2000.

[112] Quoted in Skevington Wood, *The Inextinguishable Flame*, p. 169.

[113] S.E. Dwight, "Memoirs of Jonathan Edwards" in *The Works of Jonathan Edwards, Volume 1*, London, 1840, p. xcix.

[114] For an excellent introduction to Thomas Boston and the issues involved in the Marrow Controversy, see A.T.B. McGowan, *The Federal Theology of Thomas Boston*, Rutherford Studies in Historical Theology, Paternoster Press, 1997.

[115] He is not to be confused with his son of the same name, who founded the Relief Church in 1761.

[116] John Macleod, *Scottish Theology,* Edinburgh 1943, p. 146.

[117] Macleod, *Scottish Theology*, p. 145.

The Nineteenth Century – Mission

[118] H.H. Rowdon, 'Hudson Taylor,' *Lion History*, p. 554.

[119] See also the biography of Hudson Taylor by J. Cromarty, *It is Not Death to Die*, Christian Focus Publications, 2000.

[120] For a biography and diary extracts, letters and sermons, see M. McMullen, *God's Polished Arrow*, Christian Focus Publications, 2000.

[121] For further reading see R. Mackenzie, *David Livingstone*, Christian Focus Publications, 2000.

[122] There are some useful reviews of these developments in the nineteenth century Scottish church, such as Douglas Ansdell *The People of the Great Faith: The Highland Church 1690-1900*, Stornoway, 1998, and James L. Macleod, *The Second Disruption: the Free Church in Victorian Scotland and the Origins of the Free Presbyterian Church*, Edinburgh, 2000.

[123] J.S. Andrews, 'Hymns and Church Music,' *Lion History*, p. 530.

[124] D.W. Bebbington, 'William Wilberforce,' *Lion History*, p. 561.

[125] cf. Walter Kaiser's comment that 'On the American scene, the most important contribution to the subject of inspiration, which followed in the train of thought set by the Reformation, was that of Princeton Seminary' (W.C. Kaiser, Jr., 'A Neglected Text in Bibliology Discussions: 1 Corinthians 2:6-16,' *Westminster Theological Journal*, 43:2 (Spring 1981), p. 301.

[126] J.W. Stewart in *Dictionary of the Presbyterian and Reformed Tradition in America*, IVP, 1999, p. 122. For a history of Princeton Seminary and its influence, see the two volumes on *Princeton Seminary* by D.B. Calhoun (Banner of Truth, 1994 and 1996).

[127] A.H. Freundt, Jr., *Dictionary of Presbyterian Tradition*, p. 261.

[128] Douglas Kelly, *Preachers with Power: Four Stalwarts of the South*, Banner of Truth, 1992, p. 69.

[129] Morton H. Smith, *Studies in Southern Presbyterian Theology*, New Jersey, 1987, p. 216. Smith goes on to describe Dabney as without doubt 'the greatest theologian that either Union Seminary of Virginia or Austin Seminary of Texas (both of which he served) has ever had'.

[130] Kelly, *Preachers with Power*, p. 68.

[131] R.B. Gaffin, Introduction to R.B. Gaffin (ed.), *Redemptive History and Biblical Interpretation: the Shorter Writings of Geerhardus Vos*, New Jersey, 1980, p. xiv.

The Twentieth Century – Maturity

[132] Through the writings and teachings of scholars like Thomas F. Torrance, Barthianism came to be domesticated within mainstream Scottish theology.

[133] For further discussion, see my *Doctrine of Sin*, Christian Focus Publications, 1999.

[134] W.A. Hoffecker, *Dictionary of Presbyterian Tradition*, p. 272.

[135] B.B. Warfield, 'Christian Supernaturalism', *Biblical and Theological Studies*, Philadelphia, 1952, p. 21.

[136] M. Silva, *Explorations in Exegetical Method: Galatians as a Test Case*, Baker Books, 1996, p. 215. The quotation is taken from the conclusion of his epilogue, entitled 'Reader and Relevance', which is an important discussion of the relationship between spiritual life and academic scholarship and research.

[137] For further reading and evaluation, see the perspectives of

C.R.Trueman, writing on 'The future of evangelical scholarship: A British perspective' and C.L. Blomberg, 'The past, present and future of American evangelical theological scholarship' in *Solid Ground: 25 Years of Evangelical Theology*, Apollos, 2000, pp. 291-319.

[138] See the article by Professor S.J. Brown under this title in *The Journal of Ecclesiastical History*, Vol 45, No. 1 (January 1994), pp. 82-104.

[139] For discussion and critique see Bruce A. Ware, *God's Lesser Glory: A Critique of Open Theism*, Apollos, 2000, and John M. Frame, *No Other God: A Response to Open Theism*, Presbyterian & Reformed, 2001.

[140] C. Catherwood, *Crash Course on Church History*, Hodder and Stoughton, 1998, p. 185.

[141] Introduction to the New Living Translation, Tyndale Publishers, 1996, p. xlvi.

[142] Preface to the English Standard Version, Collins, 2002, p. vii.

[143] For discussion see D.A. Carson, *The Inclusive Language Debate: A Plea for Realism*, IVP, 1998.

[144] P. Johnstone, *Operation World*, OM Publishing, 1994, p. 25.

The Challenge for the Church

[145] Noll, *Turning Points*, p.15. See Noll's Introduction for a further discussion on the importance and benefits of church history.

Great Events in the Story of the Church
Geoffrey Hanks

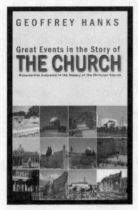

Starting with the crucifixion of Jesus, Geoffrey Hanks explains the significance of 36 key events on our church today. You'll be surprised at some of the inclusions – but amazed once you discover the dramatic effect that they have had.

Geoffrey Hanks has become a virtuoso of accessible history books. This eagerly expected volume will make you look at Church history with a new awareness and appreciation. It will also spur you on to make sure that some of the advances described in these pages are not lost for future generations.

Useful information boxes give further background details for some of the events.

Enough to whet the appetite, not enough to bore. The details are invariably well presented.

Oxford Times

A fount of information, not only about the people but about the movements which sprung up from time to time.

Our Inheritance

A wealth of material under one cover... pitched at the level of the average church member.

Scottish Baptist Magazine

A style that is both readable and easy to digest... if like me you are inquisitive and wonder how some of the movements and missions that we are so familiar with came into being, then this book is for you. I thoroughly recommend it!

Evangelism Today

A master of précis, tables, pictures, and mini-articles on men and movements ancillary to the subject being written about. Sadly, many Christians are quite ignorant about he origins of their beliefs, and the giants of their faith. The general excuse is that history is boring. Mr Hanks has removed that excuse forever. In an exciting way, he brings the past back to life, and once picked up, his book is very hard to put down - Highly commended.

Mike Adams

ISBN 1 85792 383 9

Heart of the Gospel
Meditations of Christ and the Christian Life
By Rev. John MacIver and Rev. John Mackenzie
Edited by Rev Iain D Campbell

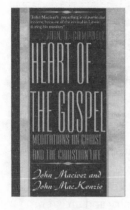

"Good sermons cannot be prepared in the last half hour of the week. They are shaped by the preacher's understanding and intellect."

Good living is also not achieved without effort but one way we can encourage ourselves is to remember the lives and witness of those in the past, to try to imitate them insofar as they copied Christ.

Our whole lifestyle should revolve round the person and work of Jesus Christ; the preaching of the God's word should also centre round the themes of Christ's work and the Christian response to that work.

The sermon notes collected here are from two men who exemplified both godly living and godly preaching. Although from similar backgrounds and related by marriage they had totally different styles; together they epitomise that art and discipline of preaching.

Whilst the full results of such preaching are impossible to measure, the ministry of John MacIver in Carloway was blessed with revival, central to which was the preaching of the word.

John MacIver was the minister of Carloway Free Church from 1924 to 1946. John MacKenzie was minister in Plockton and Kyle Free Church from 1934 till 1946 and then in Harris until 1968. Their message, as fresh and relevant today as when first preached, is as vital for our generation as it was for theirs.

ISBN 1 85792 182 8